# DESSERT ROLL
## *Quilts*  12 simple Dessert Roll quilt patterns

## Pam & Nicky Lintott

D&C
David and Charles
www.stitchcraftcreate.co.uk

# CONTENTS

# INTRODUCTION

Dessert Rolls are delicious bundles of twenty 5in wide strips cut across the width of the fabric, produced by our favourite fabric company, Moda, who never stop providing us with exactly what we want. In this book we have twelve exciting new quilts to make with dessert rolls, which we hope will inspire you to try them.

After writing eight bestselling books on jelly rolls quilts, there can be no denying our love for jelly rolls and working with strips of fabrics. Working with 5in wide strips of fabric has really captured our imagination as it opens up so many design possibilities. All the quilts in this book use just one dessert roll, so as long as you have a dessert roll or twenty 5in strips cut across the width of the fabric, you can make any of the quilts in this book. You may have to add some background fabric or border fabric and if so this is clearly stated in the Requirements for each quilt.

You know that the fabrics in your dessert roll are going to coordinate well, so if you find choosing fabrics the most difficult part of quilt making then this will make life easy for you. Even if you love choosing your own fabrics, sometimes speed is of the essence and you will find that the quilts in this book are great for that quick quilt you have to make in a hurry.

Thinking of dessert rolls whilst designing these patterns made us feel hungry, and when making quilts there is nothing better than something sweet to nibble on, so we decided to feature recipes with our patterns. When researching the recipes, we came across a file of recipes sent in by our customers nearly twenty years ago. If you recognize one of your recipes here we hope you don't mind us making it available to the quilting world at large. We've made them for our workshops so we know they taste good. Other recipes included are favourites from family and friends which are quick to make and always turn out great.

# GETTING STARTED

## WHAT IS A DESSERT ROLL?

A dessert roll is a roll of twenty fabrics cut in 5in wide strips across the width of the fabric. If you want to make any of the dessert roll quilts in this book and don't have a dessert roll to use, then cut a 5in wide strip from twenty fabrics from your stash and you can follow all the instructions in just the same way. Our patterns are based on a dessert roll strip being 42in long.

## IMPERIAL OR METRIC?

Dessert rolls from Moda are cut 5in wide and at The Quilt Room we have continued to cut our strip bundles 5in wide. When quilt making, it is impossible to mix metric and imperial measurements. It would be absurd to have a 5in strip and tell you to cut it 12.7cm to make a square! It wouldn't be square and nothing would fit. This caused a dilemma when writing instructions for our quilts and a decision had to be made. All our instructions therefore are written in inches. To convert inches to centimetres, multiply the inch measurement by 2.54. For your convenience, any extra fabric you will need, given in the Requirements panel at the start of the quilt instructions, is given in both metric and imperial.

## SEAM ALLOWANCE

We cannot stress enough the importance of maintaining an accurate scant ¼in seam allowance throughout. Please take the time to check your seam allowance with the seam allowance test at the back of the book.

## TOOLS USED

When cutting half-square triangles from strips, we use the Multi-Size 45/90 and Multi-Size 45/60 from Creative Grids, which have markings that refer to the *finished* size. If you are using a different ruler when cutting half-square triangles, please make sure you are using the correct markings before cutting.

## QUILT SIZES

In this book we have shown what can be achieved with *just one dessert roll*. We have added background fabric and borders but the basis of each quilt is just one dessert roll. The size of our quilts is therefore restricted to this fact but there is nothing to stop you using more fabric and increasing the size of your quilt. The Vital Statistics in each chapter gives you all the information you need to enable you to do some simple calculations to make a larger quilt.

## DIAGRAMS

Diagrams have been provided to help you make the quilts and these are normally beneath or beside the relevant stepped instruction. The direction in which fabric should be pressed is indicated by arrows on the diagrams. The reverse side of the fabric is shown in a lighter colour than the right side.

## WASHING NOTES

It is important that pre-cut fabric is not washed before use. Save the washing until your quilt is complete and then make use of a colour catcher in the wash or possibly dry clean.

## BEFORE YOU START

Before you dive into making a quilt please read the instructions fully and don't forget to keep that scant ¼in seam allowance. Most of all – have fun. We designed these quilts to be easy to make and we hope they will be well used and loved. The techniques we use do encourage accuracy but no one is going to be judging you on every last point!

# WEEKENDER

This is the perfect project for a weekend of sewing. By the end of the weekend you will most definitely have finished your quilt top and more than likely finished off the weekender biscuits that you have made to keep you going! We chose a plain white as our accent fabric as we didn't want to introduce another colour but a flash of yellow or red would also look great.

The variation quilt has a retro feel and its contemporary pattern certainly suits the bright, colourful fabrics selected for it.

## Recipe:

### Weekender Chocolate Biscuits
This is a really easy recipe for a weekend treat – perfect to nibble on while quilt making.

#### Ingredients
- 4oz (120g) soft margarine
- 2oz (60g) caster sugar
- 4oz (120g) plain flour
- 1 tablespoon cocoa
- ½ teaspoon vanilla essence

Cream the margarine and caster sugar and then stir in the vanilla essence. Add the sifted flour and cocoa and mix. Roll into small balls and flatten with a wet fork. Cook for 20 minutes at 170°C/325°F (gas mark 3).

# WEEKENDER QUILT

## Vital Statistics

| | |
|---|---|
| Quilt size: | 67in x 67in |
| Block size: | 11in |
| Number of blocks: | 25 |
| Setting: | 5 x 5 blocks + 6in wide border |

## Requirements

- One dessert roll **OR** twenty 5in strips cut across the width of the fabric
- 6in (15cm) of accent fabric
- 1⅜yd (1.25m) of fabric for border
- ½yd (50cm) of fabric for binding

*We chose a fun quilting design with shamrocks and swirls to enhance this quilt. We didn't want the thread to overpower the contemporary design so chose a fairly subtle colour that blended well.*

## SORTING THE STRIPS

- There is no sorting of the dessert roll strips needed, as all of the strips are cut the same way.

## CUTTING INSTRUCTIONS

*Dessert roll strips:*

- Take the twenty dessert roll strips and cut each of them as follows. You need a length of 42¼in so don't be too zealous when trimming the selvedges.
  - Cut four rectangles 5in x 7in. Keep the four rectangles from each strip together as these are for Block A.

  - Cut one square 5in x 5in.

  - Cut one rectangle 5in x 9¼in. Trim the 5in x 9¼in rectangle to measure 2¾in x 9¼in. Set these rectangles aside for Block B.

*Accent fabric:*

- Cut three 1½in wide strips across the width of the fabric.
  - Subcut each strip into seven rectangles 1½in x 6in to make twenty-one rectangles. You need twenty, so one is spare. These are the inner frames for Block B.

*Border fabric:*

- Cut seven 6½in wide strips across the width of the fabric.

*Binding fabric:*

- Cut seven 2½in wide strips across the width of the fabric.

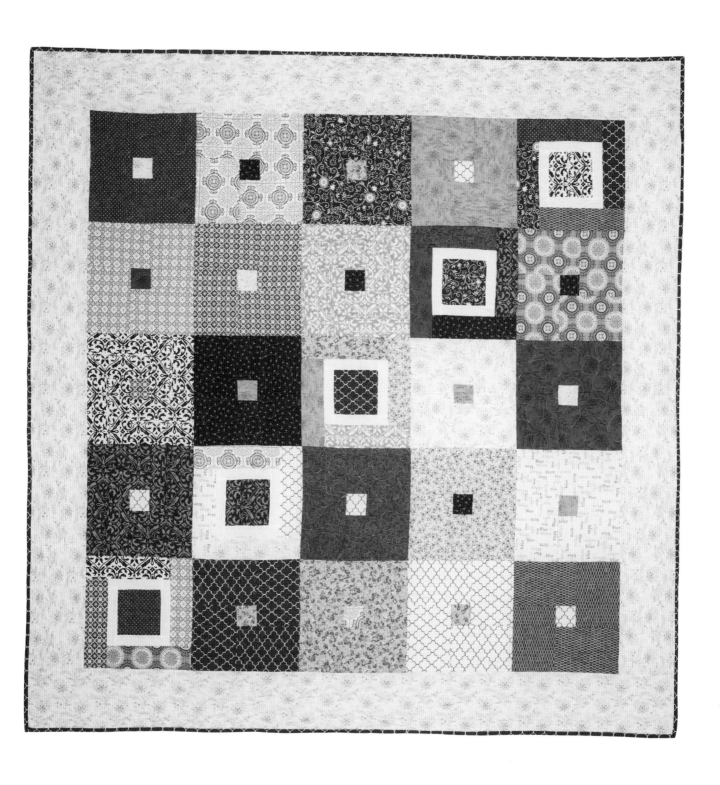

## MAKING THE CENTRE SQUARES

**1** Choose five of the 5in squares that you have cut from the dessert roll strips and subcut them in half in both directions to make twenty 2½in squares for the centres of Block A.

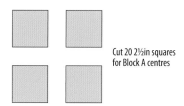

Cut 20 2½in squares
for Block A centres

**2** Choose another five 5in squares and set them aside for the centres of Block B. The remaining ten 5in squares are spare.

Choose 5 5in squares
for Block B centres

## MAKING BLOCK A

**3** Working with one set of four 5in x 7in rectangles from the same strip, take one rectangle and one 2½in centre square allocated for Block A. Place right sides together as shown and partially sew along the top seam, starting the seam approximately in the centre of the 2½in square. Carefully press open.

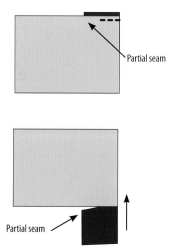

Partial seam

Partial seam

**4** Sew another 5in x 7in rectangle down the right-hand side as shown and press open.

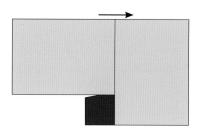

**5** In the same way sew another 5in x 7in rectangle along the bottom and press open.

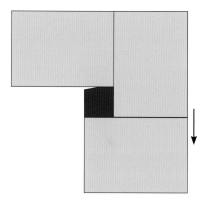

**6** Sew the fourth 5in x 7in rectangle in place and press open. Finish sewing the partial seam to complete Block A and then press. Repeat to make twenty of Block A.

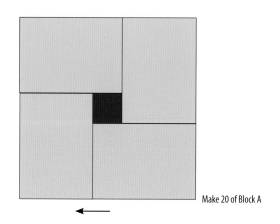

Make 20 of Block A

**9** Select four 2¾in x 9¹/4in rectangles. These blocks are going to be scrappy and we chose four rectangles of similar shade. Sew the first rectangle on with a partial seam.

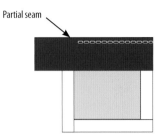

Partial seam

**10** Continue to sew all four rectangles as before, pressing before adding the next rectangle. Complete the partial seam to complete Block B. Repeat to make five of Block B.

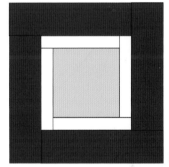

Make 5 of Block B

## MAKING BLOCK B

**7** Take one 1in x 6in rectangle of accent fabric and one 5in square and place right sides together as shown. Partially sew along the top seam. Carefully press open.

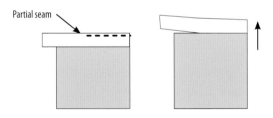

Partial seam

**8** Continue sewing four 1in x 6in rectangles around the centre square and then finish sewing the partial seam to complete Block B. Press open.

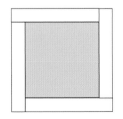

15

## ASSEMBLING THE BLOCKS

**11** Referring to the diagram, lay out the blocks into rows to make five rows of five blocks. We chose to have our five Block Bs running diagonally across the quilt. When you are happy with the layout, sew the blocks into rows and then sew the rows together. Press the seams of the first row to the left and the seams of the second row to the right (and so on), so the seams will nest together nicely when sewing the rows together.

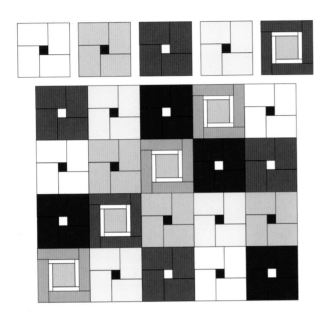

## SEWING THE BORDERS

**12** Join the seven border strips into a continuous length. Determine the vertical measurement from top to bottom through the centre of your quilt top. Cut two side borders to this measurement.

**13** Mark the halves and quarters of one quilt side and one border with pins. Placing right sides together and matching the pins, stitch the quilt and border together, easing the quilt side to fit where necessary. Repeat on the opposite side and then press seams.

**14** Determine the horizontal measurement from side to side across the centre of the quilt top. Cut two borders to this measurement. Pin and sew to the top and bottom of the quilt and press.

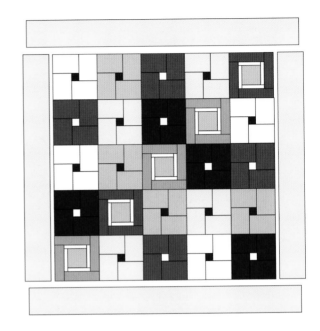

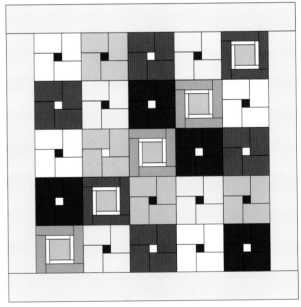

**15** The quilt top is now complete. Prepare the top, wadding (batting) and backing fabric for quilting and quilt as desired – see Quilting in the General Techniques section. Bind the quilt to finish, following the instructions in Binding a Quilt.

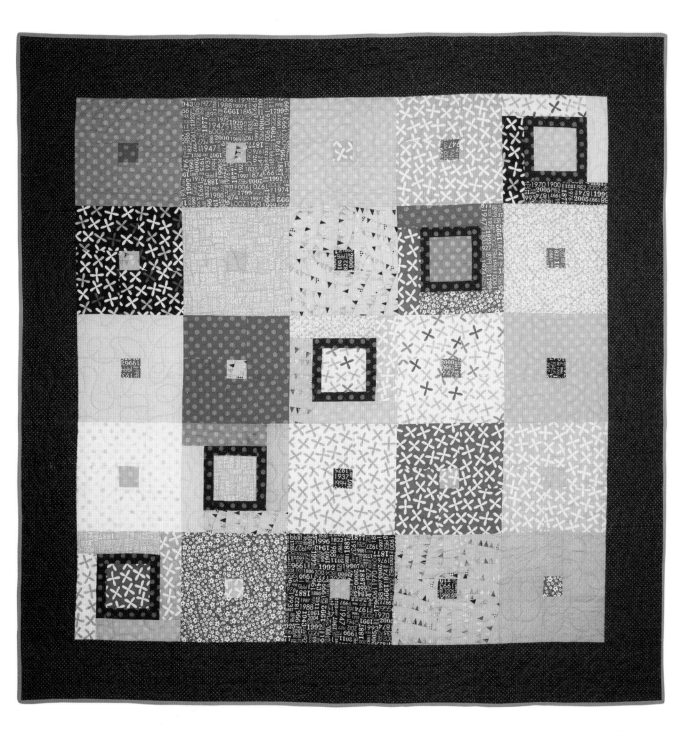

*Our variation quilt is made using some great retro fabrics from Sweetwater. This would be a wonderful quilt to give to someone heading off to college for the first time – a lovely reminder of home to snuggle under. The five B blocks are arranged diagonally across the quilt but if you prefer you could change the layout slightly by having one in the centre and the other four in the outer corners. This quilt was made by the authors and longarm quilted by The Quilt Room.*

17

# AFTERNOON TEA

Back in 1992 when Pam brought out her first book *The Quilt Room Patchwork & Quilting Workshops,* she featured a simple design that she called Melon Patch. It is a design she has always loved and here Pam and Nicky have made good use of 5in strips to recreate the design. This is a quick and simple quilt to make and looks so effective using the bright, vintage-colour palette from Tilda fabrics by Tone Finnanger. This quilt is perfect for quilters just starting out or for experienced quilters who need a quilt made quickly.

The variation quilt shown at the end of the chapter is made in aqua fabrics and really shows you that by simply moving your blocks around slightly, you can create a new quilt with a different look.

## Recipe:

### Scones

Afternoon tea is perfect with homemade scones and here's a foolproof recipe. Serve with lashings of jam and cream.

### Ingredients
- 20oz (500g) plain flour
- 1 teaspoon salt
- 2 teaspoons bicarbonate of soda
- 4½ teaspoons cream of tartar
- 2oz (50g) cold unsalted butter cut into small squares
- 1oz (25g) lard cut into small squares
- 10 fl oz (300mls) milk
- 1 large egg for glaze

Sift all dry ingredients in a large bowl. Rub in the butter. Add milk and mix briefly. Knead lightly on a floured surface to form a dough. Roll out to 1¼in (3cm) thickness. Using a 2½in (6½cm) round cutter, stamp out about twelve scones. Place on a baking tray and brush with beaten egg. Cook in pre-heated oven 220°C/425°F (gas mark 7) for 10 minutes.

# Afternoon Tea Quilt

## Vital Statistics

Quilt size:        63in x 63in
Block size:        9in
Number of blocks:  36
Setting:           6 x 6 blocks + 4½in wide border

## Requirements

- One dessert roll **OR** twenty 5in strips cut across the width of the fabric
- 2⅝yd (2.5m) of light fabric for background and border
- ½yd (50cm) of fabric for binding

## SORTING THE STRIPS

- Choose eighteen dessert roll strips for the quilt.
- Two strips are spare.

## CUTTING INSTRUCTIONS

*Dessert roll strips:*
- Cut each of the eighteen strips into eight 5in squares and keep the eight squares from each strip together. Each strip will make two blocks.

*Light fabric:*
- Cut twenty 2¾in strips across the width of the fabric. Subcut each strip into fifteen 2¾in squares to make a total of 300 2¾in squares. You need 288, so twelve are spare.
- Cut seven 5in strips across the width of the fabric and set aside for the borders.

*Binding:*
- Cut seven 2½in wide strips across the width of the fabric.

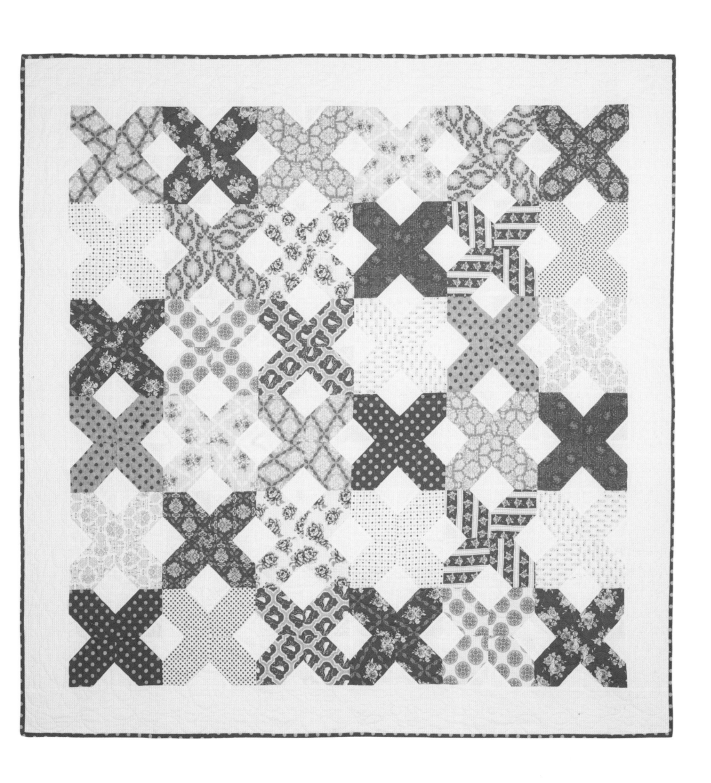

AFTERNOON TEA

## MAKING THE BLOCKS

**1** Take a 2¾in light background square and draw a diagonal line from corner to corner on the wrong side or mark the diagonal line with a fold.

**2** Working with one pile of eight dessert roll squares at a time, with right sides together, lay a marked background square on one corner of a 5in dessert roll square, aligning the outer edges. Sew across the diagonal, using the marked diagonal line as the stitching line.

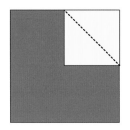

**3** Flip the square over and press towards the outside of the block. For those familiar with our books, we would normally trim the excess fabric from the flip-over corner but not trim the dessert roll square. Although this creates a little more bulk, it will help keep your patchwork in shape. However, if you find the darker fabric shows through the light corner, it may be necessary to trim the dessert roll square as well. Do not trim the dessert roll square until you have pressed the flip-over corner and you can see that it is sewn on accurately. If it is not sewn on perfectly then it is better to leave the dessert roll square uncut.

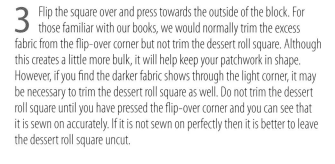

**4** Sew a second 2¾in light background square as before, on the diagonally opposite corner. Repeat with all eight dessert roll squares from the same fabric.

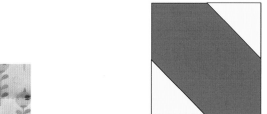

**5** Take four units and sew them together as shown, pinning at the seam intersection. Press as shown. Repeat with the other four units to make two blocks.

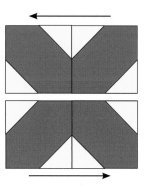

**6** Repeat steps 1–5 with the other dessert roll squares to make thirty-six blocks in total.

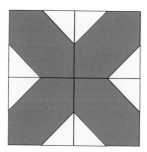

## ASSEMBLING THE QUILT

**7** Lay out the blocks into six rows of six blocks. When you are happy with the layout sew the blocks into rows and then sew the rows together, pinning at every seam intersection. Press the seams of alternate rows in opposite directions so that the seams nest together nicely when sewn together.

## ADDING THE BORDER

**8** Join your border strips into one continuous length. Determine the vertical measurement from top to bottom through the centre of your quilt top. Cut two side borders to this measurement.

**9** Mark the halves and quarters of one quilt side and one border with pins. Placing right sides together and matching the pins, stitch the quilt and border together, easing the quilt side to fit where necessary. Repeat on the opposite side and then press seams.

*We thought this looked a very girly quilt so we chose a pretty daisy quilting design and used a subtle colour of thread, which blended with both the background fabric and the lovely pink and red fabric.*

**10** Now determine the horizontal measurement from side to side across the centre of the quilt top. Cut two borders to this measurement. Sew to the top and bottom of your quilt and press.

**11** The quilt top is now complete. Prepare the top, wadding (batting) and backing fabric for quilting and quilt as desired – see Quilting in the General Techniques section. Bind the quilt to finish, following the instructions in Binding a Quilt.

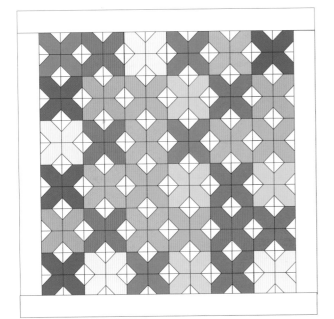

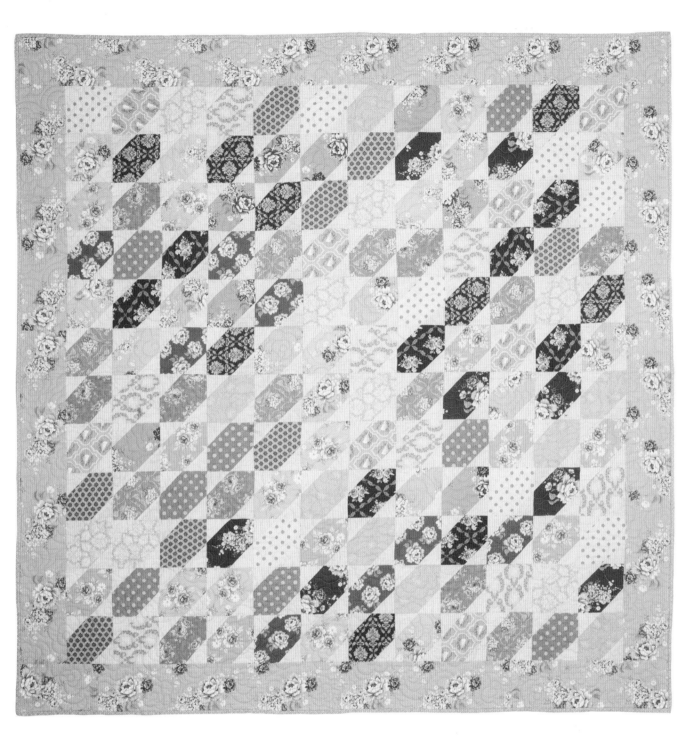

In our variation we have pieced our blocks so that all the units are facing the same way. We made the quilt far more scrappy, by just sewing the units together randomly. We also added a different coloured border and if you want to have a border fabric that is different from the background fabric you will only need 1⅝yd (1.5m) for the background and 1yd (1m) for the border fabric. Again, we have used the delightful Tilda fabric but this time in a blue and green colourway. The quilt was made by the authors and longarm quilted by The Quilt Room.

# ORANGE SQUEEZE

This quilt features a simple four-patch block set on point with sashing and sashing squares. Just add an extra 3¼yd (3m) of background fabric and you have a great bed-size quilt in no time at all. If you haven't set blocks on point before then here is your chance. The 5in strips from the dessert roll make the blocks easy to piece and then it is just a matter of setting the blocks on point to complete the quilt. We used the colourful fabrics from Honey Honey by Kate Spain coupled with a coordinating blue from the Moda Crackle range.

For the variation quilt we stepped up the colour combinations with bright floral fabrics combined with a lovely purple for the sashing.

## Recipe:

### Orange Squeeze Cake

**Ingredients**
- 1 orange
- 3 eggs
- 8oz (230g) caster sugar
- 9oz (255g) ground almonds
- ½ teaspoon baking powder

Boil the orange for an hour and then liquidize the whole orange. Beat the eggs with the sugar. Add the orange, ground almonds and baking powder and mix well. Put the mixture in an 8in (20cm) diameter tin and cook for 45–50 minutes at 180ºC/350ºF (gas mark 4).

# ORANGE SQUEEZE QUILT

## Vital Statistics

Quilt size:              66in x 82in
Block size:              9in
Number of blocks:        32 blocks
Setting:                 On point with 2in sashing and
                         2in sashing squares

## Requirements

- One dessert roll **OR** twenty 5in strips cut across
  the width of the fabric
- 3¼yd (3m) of background fabric
- The binding is made from the dessert roll strips

## SORTING THE STRIPS

- Sixteen strips for the four-patch blocks, paired up into eight pairs.
  Try to pair a light with a dark strip but do not worry too much if there
  isn't a lot of contrast.
- Four strips for the sashing squares and the binding.

## CUTTING INSTRUCTIONS

*Dessert roll strips:*

- Leave the sixteen strips allocated for the four-patch blocks uncut.
- Take the four strips allocated for the sashing squares and the binding
  and cut in half lengthways to make eight strips 2½in x about 42in.
  – From three of the 2½in wide strips you need to cut forty-nine
    2½in squares, so cut sixteen 2½in squares from two of the strips
    and then cut seventeen from the third strip. This is a little tight so
    do not trim your selvedges too much.
  – From the remaining five 2½in strips, cut in half to form ten 2½in x
    21in rectangles and set aside for the binding.

*Background fabric:*

- Cut twenty-three 2½in wide strips across the width of the fabric.
  – Take twenty of these 2½in strips and subcut each into four
    rectangles 2½in x 9½in to make a total of eighty sashing strips.
  – Take three 2½in strips and cut in half to form six 2½in x 21in
    rectangles and set aside for the binding.
- Cut two 18in strips across the width of the fabric and subcut each
  strip into two squares to make four 18in squares. Cut across both
  diagonals of each square to make a total of sixteen setting triangles.
  You need fourteen, so two are spare.

18in square

- Cut one strip 12in wide and subcut two 12in squares. Cut across one
  diagonal of each square to make four corner triangles. Cutting the
  setting and corner triangles in this way ensures that there are no bias
  edges on the outside of your quilt.

12in square

# MAKING THE FOUR-PATCH UNITS

**1** Take one pair of dessert roll strips and lay them right sides together. Sew down the long side. Open and press towards the darker fabric. Repeat with the remaining pairs of strips to make a total of eight strip units.

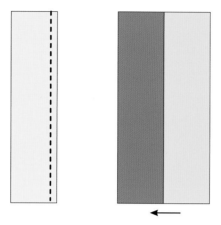

**2** Taking two strip units, with right sides together, lay one strip unit on top of another, reversing the position of the light and dark strips. Ensure that the centre seams are in alignment.

**3** Use your quilter's ruler to subcut this strip-pieced unit into eight 5in wide segments.

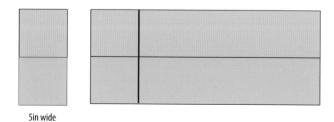

5in wide

**4** Carefully keeping the pairs together, sew down the long side as shown, pinning at the seam intersection to ensure a perfect match. The seams will nest together nicely as they are pressed in different directions. Chain piece for speed. Press open to form eight four-patch units.

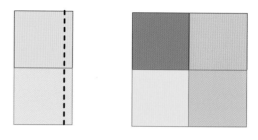

**5** Repeat this process with the remaining strips to make a total of thirty-two four-patch units.

# ASSEMBLING THE BLOCKS

**6** Sew two sashing strips to both sides of a four-patch block. Press as shown. Repeat to make twenty.

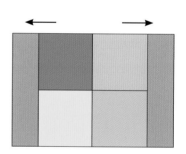

**7** Sew two sashing squares to both ends of a sashing strip. Press as shown in the diagram. Repeat to make twenty.

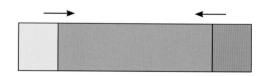

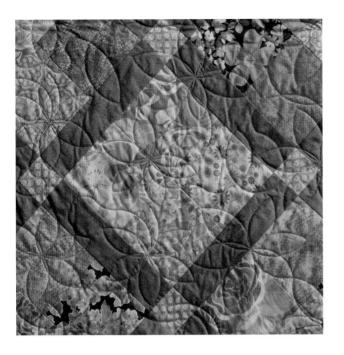

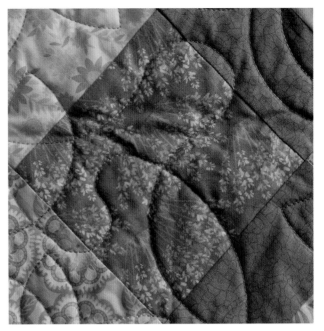

**8** Sew these two units together, pinning at the seam intersections to ensure a perfect match. Press as shown. Repeat to make twenty.

Make 20

**9** Sew one sashing strip to the top of a four-patch block. Press as shown. Repeat to make twelve.

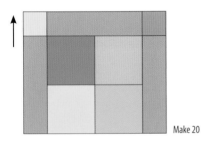

Make 12

**10** Sew eight sashing strips together with nine sashing squares as shown to form the extra row required between row 4 and row 5. Press towards the sashing squares.

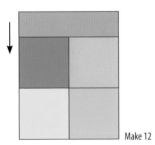

## ASSEMBLING THE QUILT

**11** Referring to the quilt layout diagram, lay out your blocks into rows. When you are happy with the arrangement, start with row 1 and sew the blocks into rows with a setting triangle at both ends, as shown in the diagram below. Press as shown. Don't sew the corner triangles on yet. The setting triangles are cut slightly larger to make the blocks 'float', so when sewing these on make sure the bottom of the triangle is aligned with the bottom of the block.

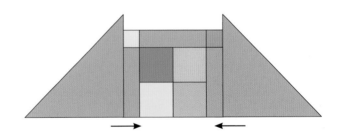

**12** Sew the rows together, pinning at every seam intersection to ensure a perfect match. Insert the extra row of sashing strips between rows 4 and 5 as shown in the diagram. Sew the four corner triangles on last.

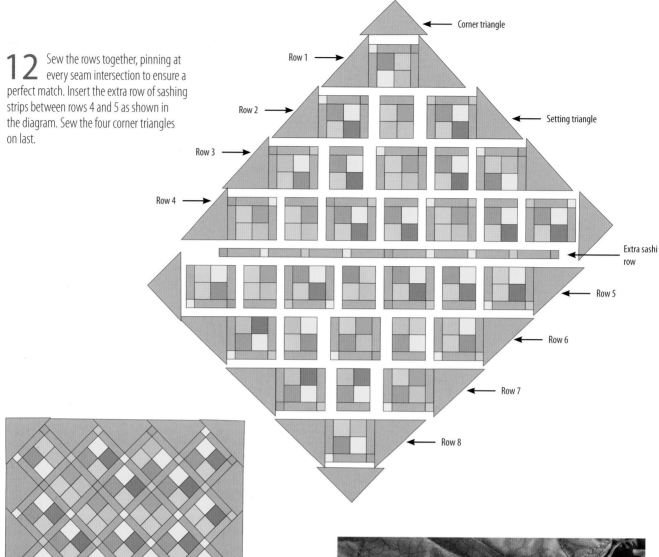

Corner triangle

Row 1

Row 2

Setting triangle

Row 3

Row 4

Extra sashi row

Row 5

Row 6

Row 7

Row 8

**13** The quilt top is now complete. Prepare the top, wadding (batting) and backing fabric for quilting and quilt as desired – see Quilting in the General Techniques section. Bind the quilt to finish, following the instructions in Binding a Quilt.

To make the scrappy binding, sew the ten 2½in x 21in dessert roll rectangles alternating with the six 2½in x 21in background rectangles to make a continuous length. You need a length of approximately 310in.

*With all the bright floral prints in this quilt we decided on a flower quilting design, which weaves its way cheerfully across the quilt.*

Our variation uses the fabulously bold floral fabrics designed by Philip Jacobs for Westminster Fabrics and we added even more zing to the quilt by mixing them with a light purple to bring out their gorgeous colours. The quilt was made by the authors and longarm quilted by The Quilt Room.

# ROCK 'N' ROLL

Simply created from rows of 60 degree triangles and two easy borders, you will find that this quilt looks great whatever fabrics you choose to use. We have used the sophisticated colouring of Japanese taupes with a splash of red for our main quilt, which creates a very smart and stylish look and would be great as a present for the man in your life.

See how stunning the variation quilt looks, made with the bright, fresh colours of Gypsy Girl by Lily Ashbury for Moda. The splash of blues creates a wonderful contrast with all the warm terracotta shades.

## Recipe:

### Rock Buns
This is an old classic that never loses its charm.

#### Ingredients
- 12oz (350g) self-raising flour
- Pinch of salt
- ¼ teaspoon grated nutmeg
- ¼ teaspoon mixed spice
- 6oz (180g) butter or margarine
- 6oz (180g) sugar
- 3oz (90g) currants
- 1½oz (50g) chopped peel
- 1 egg
- Milk to mix

Sift the flour, salt and spices. Rub in the fat and add the sugar, fruit and peel. Mix with a beaten egg and enough milk to bind. Put in rocky heaps on a greased baking tray and bake for 15–20 minutes at 200°C/400°F (gas mark 6).

# Rock 'n' Roll Quilt

## Vital Statistics

Quilt size: 57in x 69in
Setting: 12 rows of 17 triangles each
+ 1½in inner border and 6in
outer border

## Requirements

- One dessert roll **OR** twenty 5in strips cut across the width of the fabric
- ⅜yd (40cm) of fabric for inner border
- 1½yd (1.25m) of fabric for outer border
- ½yd (50cm) of fabric for binding
- 60-degree triangle ruler or Multi-Size 45/60 triangle

## SORTING THE STRIPS

- Divide the dessert roll strips into ten dark strips and ten light strips. If some dark strips have to be allocated as lights that is fine as this will create a secondary design of larger, darker triangles within the pattern.

## CUTTING INSTRUCTIONS

*Inner border fabric:*
- Cut six 2in strips across the width of the fabric.

*Outer border fabric:*
- Cut seven 6½in strips across the width of the fabric.

*Binding fabric:*
- Cut seven 2½in strips across the width of the fabric.

ROCK 'N' ROLL

## CUTTING THE TRIANGLES

**1** Open up one dark strip and place it right side up on the cutting mat. Place the 60-degree triangle on the left side of the strip unit as shown, aligning the 5in line of the triangle with the bottom of the strip and the cut-off top of the triangle with the top of the strip. Cut your first triangle.

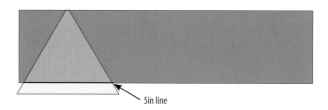

5in line

**2** Rotate the triangle ruler 180 degrees and cut the second triangle. Continue to the end of the strip rotating the ruler and cutting to make eleven triangles.

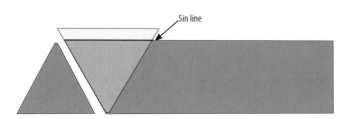

5in line

**3** Repeat with all dark and light dessert roll strips to make eleven triangles from each 5in dessert roll strip. You can layer more than one strip at a time when cutting but don't cut too many together as you will lose accuracy. You will have 110 light triangles and 110 dark triangles. You need 102 of each, so eight of each are spare.

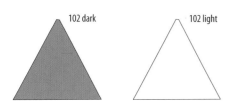

102 dark          102 light

## SEWING THE ROWS TOGETHER

**4** Take a dark and a light triangle, place right sides together and sew together. Press as shown in the diagram.

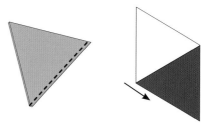

**5** Take another light triangle and sew in place as shown. Press, checking that you are keeping a straight edge to your row.

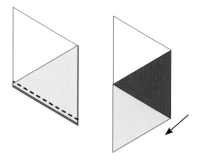

**6** Repeat, sewing seventeen triangles together alternating light and dark triangles, starting the top with a light triangle and finishing with a light triangle. Press all seams downwards. Make six of these rows.

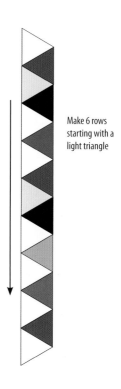

Make 6 rows starting with a light triangle

**7** Repeat to make a further six rows starting with a dark triangle and finishing with a dark triangle. Again, press all seams downwards.

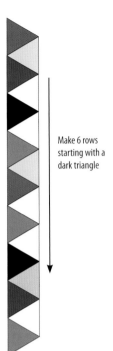

Make 6 rows starting with a dark triangle

**9** Now sew the remaining pairs of rows together to complete the centre of your quilt top.

**8** Take one row starting with a light triangle and one row starting with a dark triangle. Rotate the row starting with a dark triangle 180 degrees and sew the pair of rows together as shown, pinning at every seam intersection. Repeat with all six pairs of rows. Press as shown.

## ADDING THE BORDERS

**10** Rotate your quilt top 90 degrees to the right, so the top of the quilt is now positioned correctly. Join your 2in inner border strips into one continuous length. Determine the vertical measurement from top to bottom through the centre of your quilt top. Join, and cut two side borders to this measurement. Pin and sew to the sides of the quilt to form a straight edge. Press and then trim the excess fabric.

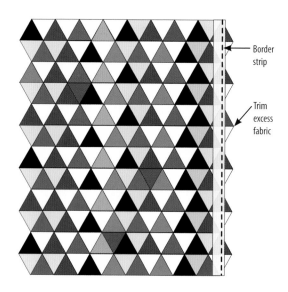

Border strip

Trim excess fabric

**11** Determine the horizontal measurement from side to side across the centre of the quilt top. Cut two inner borders to this measurement. Sew to the top and bottom of your quilt and press.

**12** Repeat this measuring process and then sew on the outer borders, sides first and then the top and bottom.

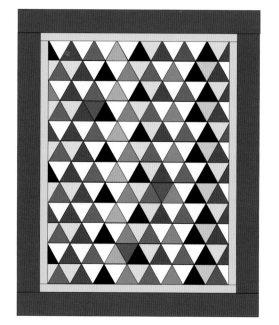

**13** The quilt top is now complete. Prepare the top, wadding (batting) and backing fabric for quilting and quilt as desired – see Quilting in the General Techniques section. Bind the quilt to finish, following the instructions in Binding a Quilt.

*With all the straight lines in this geometric patchwork pattern we wanted a quilting design with curves and swirls to create contrast and interest. We decided on a dark taupe thread that allowed the quilting design to show up well on both the light and dark fabrics.*

*Our variation shows how good the quilt looks with different fabrics. We used the bright, fresh colours of Gypsy Girl by Lily Ashbury with a lovely bright blue outer border. The quilt was made by Sheila Andrews and longarm quilted by The Quilt Room.*

# SUGAR 'N' SPICE

The technique used for this quilt is slightly unusual but great fun and your quilt will speed together in no time at all. The addition of the pieced border makes sure that absolutely nothing is wasted from the dessert roll. The range of fabric we used is Cameo by Amy Butler and includes a lovely array of blues and greens, and combined with the distinctive coral it proved to be a very effective mix.

The variation quilt uses a pretty collection of 1930s reproduction fabrics with a pink accent to create a lovely nostalgic look.

## Recipe:

### Tea Bread
The fruit, nuts and spices in this recipe make this a very tasty treat.

#### Ingredients
- 8 fl oz (230ml) milk
- 2oz (60g) chopped walnuts
- 3½oz (100g) demerara sugar
- ½ teaspoon salt
- ½ teaspoon mixed spice
- 5oz (140g) sultanas
- 2 tablespoons golden syrup
- 8oz (230g) self-raising flour
- ½ teaspoon bicarbonate of soda

Place all the ingredients in a bowl and mix together. Put in a 2lb (900g) lined loaf tin and cook for one hour at 190°C/375°F (gas mark 5). Leave to cool slightly before slicing, and buttering!

# SUGAR 'N' SPICE QUILT

## Vital Statistics

| | |
|---|---|
| Quilt size: | 78½in x 78½in |
| Block size: | 17½in |
| Number of blocks: | 9 |
| Setting: | 3 x 3 blocks + 2in sashing strips, 4½in pieced border and 4½in outer border |

## Requirements

- One dessert roll **OR** twenty 5in strips cut across the width of the fabric
- 1½yd (1.40m) of accent fabric
- 2¼yd (2.10m) of fabric for sashing and border
- ⅝yd (60cm) of fabric for binding

## SORTING THE STRIPS

- Divide the dessert roll strips into five sets of four strips each. Each set of four strips will make two blocks.
- There will be one block spare which could be used for a matching pillow.

## CUTTING INSTRUCTIONS

*Accent fabric:*
- Cut ten 5in strips across the width of the fabric.

*Sashing and border fabric:*
- Fold the fabric *lengthways* and cut eight 2½in wide strips down the *length* of the fabric.
  - Set four aside for the horizontal sashing, to be trimmed to size later.
  - Subcut each of the four remaining strips into three 2½in x 18in rectangles to make a total of twelve rectangles for the vertical sashing.
- Cut four 5in wide strips down the *length* of the fabric for the outer border.

*Binding:*
- Cut eight 2½in wide strips across the width of the fabric.

## MAKING THE BLOCKS

**1** Working with one set of four dessert roll strips at a time and two accent fabric strips, sew two strip units together as shown in the diagrams, with the accent fabric strip in the centre. Press seams in one direction. Measure the width of your strip units – they should be 14in. If not then you must adjust your seam allowance and re-sew.

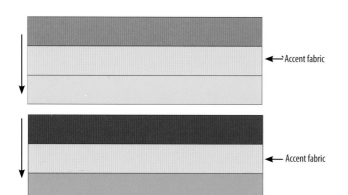

← Accent fabric

← Accent fabric

**2** Subcut each strip unit into two 14in squares. Cut the remainder of the strip unit into two 5in strips and set aside for the pieced border.

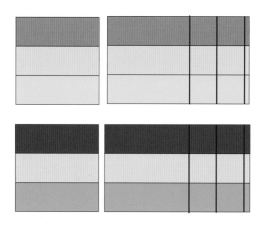

**3** Take one square from each strip unit. Rotate one square 90 degrees and place them right sides together, aligning the edges. Pin to hold them in place. Repeat with the other two squares, rotating them in the same way.

**4** Take the units to the sewing machine and, with a ¼in seam allowance, sew around the outside of all four sides of the squares.

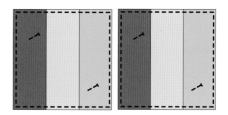

**5** Now cut through both diagonals of both squares as shown in the diagrams below.

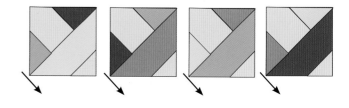

**6** Open one square to create four quarter blocks. Press in the direction shown, pressing gently as you are dealing with bias edges and need to avoid stretching the fabric.

**7** Rotate the quarter blocks as shown in the diagram. Pin and sew the top two quarters together, pressing the seam to the left. Sew the bottom two quarters together, pressing the seam to the right. Complete the blocks by sewing the two halves together, pinning at the seams to ensure a perfect match.

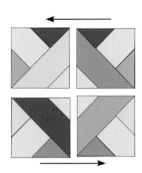

**8** Open and press the quarter squares from the other square and repeat to complete a second block. Measure your blocks — they should be 18in square. If not, trim them to size using a large quilting square.

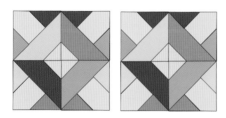

**9** Repeat with the other sets of four dessert roll strips to make a total of ten blocks. Only nine blocks are required for the quilt, so one block will be spare.

## ASSEMBLING THE QUILT

**10** Lay out all of the blocks and when you are happy with the arrangement sew three blocks together to form one row, with a sashing strip in between the blocks and a sashing strip on both sides. Repeat to make three rows like this.

**11** Measure the width of the rows and trim the horizontal sashing strips to that measurement. Sew the rows together with the sashing strips in between the rows and at the top and bottom.

## ADDING THE BORDERS

**12** Sew five sets of 5in pieced border strips together for a side border. Carefully unpick one square so that you have a row of fourteen squares (keep the square). Repeat to make two side borders. *Note:* your border strips are about 1in longer than the sides of your quilt top and will need to be adjusted. Your quilt will look nicer if the corner squares match neatly, so if you increase the size of your seam allowance to ½in when joining the pieced border strips this will take up the 1in that needs to be lost.

**13** Sew five sets of pieced border strips together for the top border. Add the discarded square from the side border so you have a row of sixteen squares. Repeat to make the bottom border.

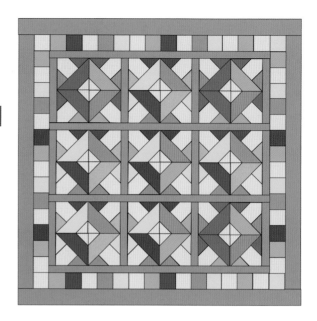

**14** Pin and sew the side borders to the quilt, easing if necessary. Press the seams. Pin and sew the top and bottom borders and press.

**17** The quilt top is now complete. Prepare the top, wadding (batting) and backing fabric for quilting and quilt as desired — see Quilting in the General Techniques section. Bind the quilt to finish, following the instructions in Binding a Quilt.

**15** Determine the vertical measurement from top to bottom through the centre of your quilt top. Trim two outer borders to this measurement. Pin and sew to the quilt, easing if necessary. Press the seams.

**16** Now determine the horizontal measurement from side to side across the centre of the quilt top. Trim two outer borders to this measurement. Pin and sew to the top and bottom of your quilt and press.

*This quilt uses a lot of busy fabrics so we chose a quilting pattern with gentle curves to create a calming effect and used a pale blue thread, which worked well with the fabrics.*

*Our variation quilt uses a pretty1930s reproduction bundle of fabrics, which we teamed with a pink accent fabric and a white for the sashing and borders. We have also arranged the colouring in the blocks slightly differently in this variation quilt. The quilt was made by the authors and longarm quilted by The Quilt Room.*

# PAVLOVA

When we met the talented Tula Pink and saw her stunning collection of fabrics we were determined to use one of her ranges in a quilt for this book. We chose the brilliant range The Birds and the Bees, and used a lime green sashing to set off the colours. This quilt pattern really lends itself to big, bold and quirky designs, which makes it a perfect pattern to showcase some gorgeous fabrics. This quilt has absolutely no seams to match up – sounds too good to be true but it is!

The variation quilt looks just as impressive using traditional fabrics, especially when teamed with a bold-coloured pink sashing.

## Recipe:

### Pear Pavlova
This delicious recipe is a firm favourite in Nicky's household!

#### Ingredients
- 6 egg whites
- 12oz (350g) caster sugar
- 3 teaspoons cornflour

#### Topping
- 10 fl oz (300ml) whipped cream
- 2 to 3 ripe pears
- Grated chocolate

Whip the egg whites at moderate speed until they are shiny and thick. Add the sugar in two batches. Whisk for a minute or so until thick and glossy. Fold in the cornflour. Put into a lined cake tin and bake for one hour at 170°C/325°F (gas mark 3) and leave in the oven to cool (don't open the door). Run a palette knife around the edges and remove from the tin. Spread on the whipped cream, top with peeled and sliced pears and sprinkle on some chocolate.

# Pavlova Quilt

## Vital Statistics

Quilt size:                  60in x 85in
Number of blocks:     96 45-degree diamonds
Setting:                     Eight vertical rows of twelve diamonds + 4in sashing and 6in borders

## Requirements

- One dessert roll **OR** twenty 5in strips cut across the width of the fabric
- 2⅛yd (2m) fabric for sashing and border
- ½yd (50cm) fabric for binding

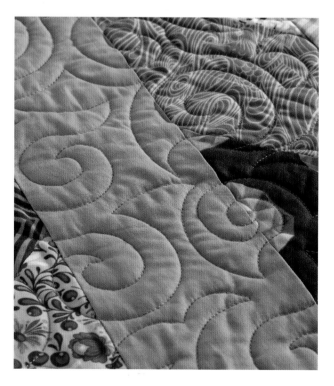

## SORTING THE STRIPS

- Ten assorted strips for the left-hand vertical row.
- Ten assorted strips for the right-hand vertical row.
- It is not necessary to divide the strips into lights or darks but sorting them in this way ensures you have different fabrics in the left-hand and right-hand rows.

## CUTTING INSTRUCTIONS

*Dessert roll strips:*

- Take one strip and, using your quilting ruler, cut the strip at a 45-degree angle as shown in the diagram.

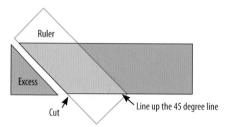

- Lining up your quilting ruler on the 45-degree cut edge, cut a 5in segment, making sure you are keeping the cut at a 45-degree angle.

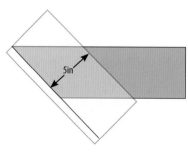

- Repeat to cut five diamonds from each of the twenty strips to make a total of fifty for the left-hand vertical rows and fifty for the right-hand vertical rows. You need forty-eight of each so you will have two spare from each side.

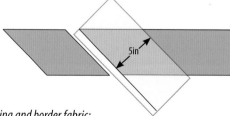

*Sashing and border fabric:*

- Fold the fabric *lengthways* and cut the following. (Cutting the fabric lengthways ensures you won't have joins in the sashing and borders.)
  – Three 4½in strips lengthways down the fabric for the sashing.
  – Four 6½in strips *lengthways* down the fabric for the borders.

*Binding fabric:*

- Cut seven 2½in strips across the width of the fabric.

## MAKING THE LEFT-HAND VERTICAL ROWS

**1** Take two diamonds and place right sides together as shown in the diagram. You will notice there is a ¼in overlap at each end – this is because you have an angled cut.

**2** Sew the diamonds together and gently press the seams downwards. Do not use steam. Check that your sewn diamonds create a straight edge. If not, then you need to check you have a ¼in overlap at each end.

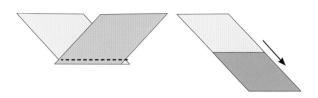

**3** Continue sewing twelve diamonds together to make one left-hand vertical row. Make four left-hand vertical rows. Treat the diamonds gently at all times as they have bias edges and can be pulled out of shape.

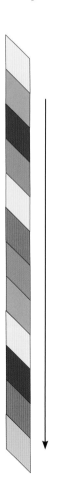

## MAKING THE RIGHT-HAND VERTICAL ROWS

**4** Take two diamonds and place them right sides together as shown. You will notice there is a ¼in overlap at each end – this is because you have an angled cut. As before, sew the diamonds together and press the seams gently downwards. Check that your sewn diamonds create a straight edge. If not, check you have a ¼in overlap at each end.

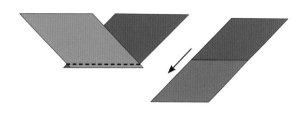

**5** Continue sewing twelve diamonds together to make one right-hand vertical row. Make four right-hand vertical rows.

## ASSEMBLING THE QUILT

6 Take one left-hand and one right-hand row and position the top diamond of the right-hand row 2in down from the top diamond of the left-hand row. Place rows right sides together and pin in place.

7 Sew the rows together, being very careful not to stretch the diamonds. Having the rows staggered like this means that there are no seams to match up at all. Press gently (don't use steam). Repeat to make a total of four double rows.

8 Trim all four rows to straighten the top and bottom. At this stage measure the rows carefully and make sure all the rows measure the same. They will be approximately 71in.

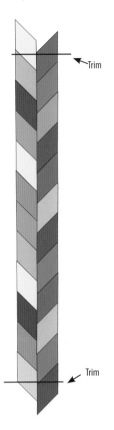

Trim

Trim

9 Take the three 4½in wide sashing strips and two 6½in border strips and trim to the exact length of your rows. It is important that they are all cut the same length.

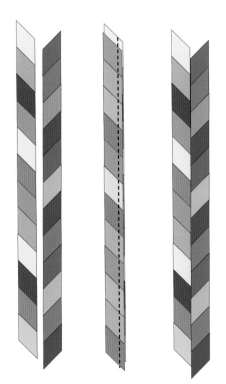

**10** Pin and sew the four vertical rows together as shown in the diagram, with the sashing in between and the border strips on each side. Take care not to stretch your fabric as you are still dealing with bias edges.

**12** The quilt top is now complete. Prepare the top, wadding (batting) and backing fabric for quilting and quilt as desired – see Quilting in the General Techniques section. Bind the quilt to finish, following the instructions in Binding a Quilt.

**11** Determine the horizontal measurement from side to side across the centre of the quilt top. Cut the remaining two 6½in border strips to this measurement. Sew to the top and bottom of your quilt and press.

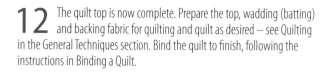

*We chose an evenly spaced swirl pattern called Deb's Swirls and used a green thread to coordinate. The design created a lovely textured effect and you can really see the pretty details of the design in the plain sashing fabric.*

*We went for a much more traditional look with our variation and used a range called Bella Bliss from Makower. We did 'zing' it up a bit with the bright pink sashing and really liked the effect. The quilt was made by the authors and longarm quilted by The Quilt Room.*

# HIGHLAND FLING

This quilt goes together very quickly and is a great one to make for that quick gift you need in a hurry. Our main quilt uses the beautiful colouring of a range called Tea Cups by Verna Mosquera, which created a very stylish quilt. The blocks tilting to the left and to the right create a nice sense of movement in the quilt.

In our variation quilt we fussy cut animals for the block centres, which would make the quilt perfect as a present for a child. You could also have plain squares for the block centres and embroider something special in them or even add appliqué letters.

*Recipe:*

## Shortbread

We named our quilt Highland Fling in honour of our Scottish heritage. Shortbread is a traditional Scottish recipe, which we thought was the perfect choice for a highland fling!

### Ingredients
- 6oz (170g) plain flour
- 2oz (60g) semolina
- 3oz (85g) caster sugar
- 6oz (170g) diced butter

Sieve the flour and add the semolina and sugar. Add the butter and mix to fine crumbs. In a bowl, work the mixture into a dough. Spread out to ½in (1.3cm) thick on a floured board. Prick with a fork and place on a lightly greased tray about 7in x 11in (18cm x 28cm). Bake for 30 minutes at 180°C/350°F (gas mark 4). Cut into slices while still warm.

# HIGHLAND FLING QUILT

## Vital Statistics

| | |
|---|---|
| Quilt size: | 59½in x 69in |
| Block size: | 9½in |
| Number of blocks: | 30 |
| Setting: | 5 x 6 blocks + 1in inner border and 5in outer border |

## Requirements

- One dessert roll **OR** twenty 5in strips cut across the width of the fabric
- ⅞yd (75cm) of fabric for inner border and binding
- 1yd (1m) of fabric for outer border

## SORTING THE STRIPS

- Choose four dark strips for the block centres.
- Choose fifteen strips for the frames.
- One strip is spare.

## CUTTING INSTRUCTIONS

*Dessert roll strips:*

- Take the four strips allocated for the block centres and cut each strip into eight 5in squares. You need thirty in total, so two are spare.
- Take the fifteen strips allocated for the frames and cut each strip into four rectangles 5in x 10in.

*Inner border and binding fabric:*

- Cut six 1½in strips across the width of the fabric for the inner border.
- Cut seven 2½in strips across the width of the fabric and set aside for the binding.

*Outer border fabric:*

- Cut six 5½in strips across the width of the fabric for the outer border.

61

HIGHLAND FLING

## MAKING THE BLOCKS –
## TILTING SQUARES TO THE RIGHT

**1** Take two 5in x 10in rectangles cut from the same dessert roll strip. With right sides up, cut each rectangle diagonally from the bottom-right corner to the top-left corner as shown in the diagram. *Note*: the right angle on your triangles is on the right-hand side – this is how you know that cutting in this direction will tilt your blocks to the right.

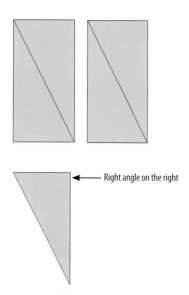

← Right angle on the right

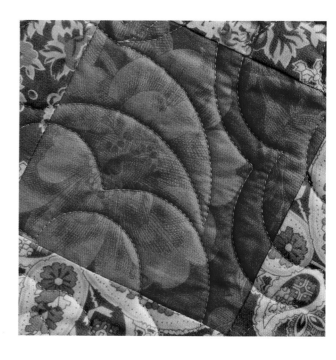

**3** Sew a triangle across the top, lining up the corners as shown. Press open. Don't worry about overlapping triangle points as you will trim the block later.

**2** Sew one triangle to the left-hand side of a centre square as shown, lining up the corners and *only sewing halfway down* the triangle. Press the triangle open. It is important to always press gently and do not use steam as these triangles have bias edges. *Note*: this triangle is only partially seamed.

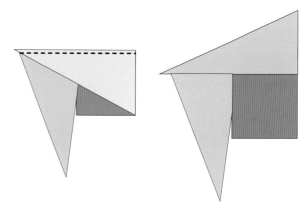

**4** Sew the next two triangles in the same manner and then complete the sewing of the first seam.

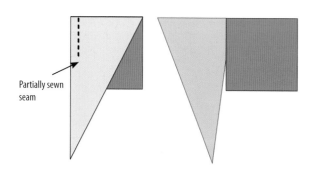

Partially sewn seam

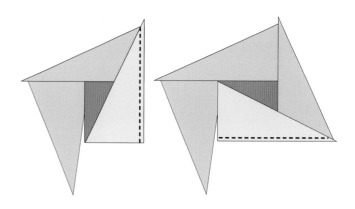

**5** Press the block open and square it up to measure 10in square. *Note*: if your block is less than 10in, this means that your seam allowance is a little wide but it won't matter as long as you square *all* the blocks to the same measurement. You need to make a total of fifteen blocks tilting to the right.

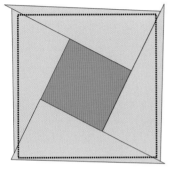

Make 15 blocks tilting to the right

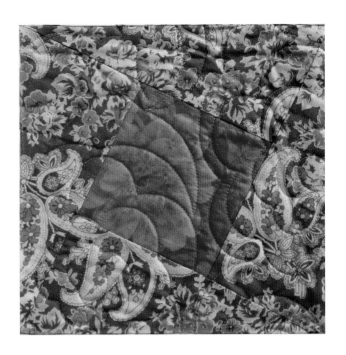

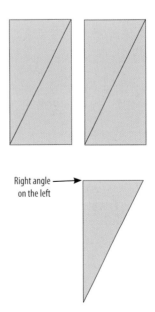

## MAKING THE BLOCKS –
## TILTING SQUARES TO THE LEFT

**6** To make the centre squares tilt to the left, take two 5in x 10in rectangles cut from the same dessert roll strip. With right sides up, cut each rectangle diagonally from the bottom-left corner to the top-right corner as shown. Notice the right angle of the triangle is now on the left-hand side.

Right angle on the left

**9** Sew the next two triangles in the same manner and then complete the sewing of the first seam.

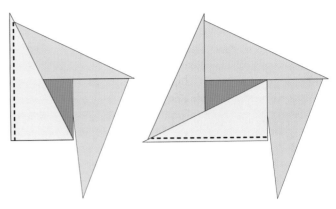

**10** Press the block open and square it up to measure 10in square. In total you need fifteen blocks tilting to the left.

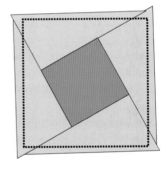

Make 15 blocks tilting to the left

**7** Sew one triangle to the right-hand side of a centre square as shown, starting with a partial seam. Line up the right-angled corner of the triangle with the corner of the centre square.

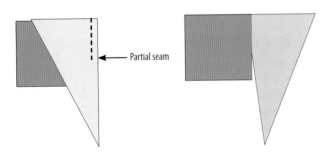

← Partial seam

**8** Sew a triangle across the top of the square, lining up the corners as shown. This time you will be adding triangles in an anti-clockwise direction.

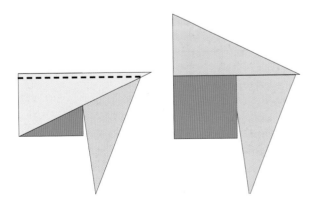

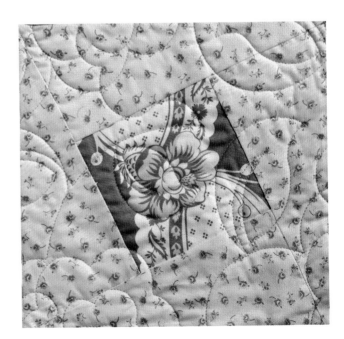

## ASSEMBLING THE QUILT

**11** Lay out the blocks alternating the blocks tilting to the right and the blocks tilting to the left. When you are happy with the layout sew the blocks into rows and then sew the rows together, pinning at every intersection to ensure a perfect match. Press the seams of alternate rows in opposite directions so they will nest together nicely when sewing the rows together. It is not necessary to try and align all the other seams.

**12** Sew the rows together and press your work. Remember that you still have bias edges on the outside of your quilt so press gently and do not use steam.

## ADDING THE BORDERS

**13** Join your 1½in wide inner border strips together to form a long length. Determine the vertical measurement from top to bottom through the centre of your quilt top. Cut the two inner side borders to this measurement. Pin and sew to the quilt and then press.

**14** Determine the horizontal measurement from side to side across the centre of the quilt top. Trim these two borders to this measurement. Pin and sew to the quilt and then press.

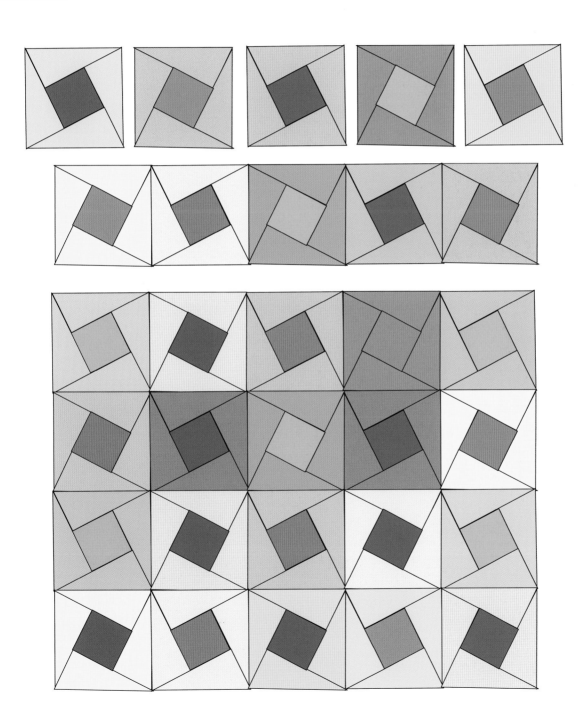

**15** Repeat this process with the 5½in wide outer border strips and then sew on the outer borders and press.

**16** The quilt top is now complete. Prepare the top, wadding (batting) and backing fabric for quilting and quilt as desired – see Quilting in the General Techniques section. Bind the quilt to finish, following the instructions in Binding a Quilt.

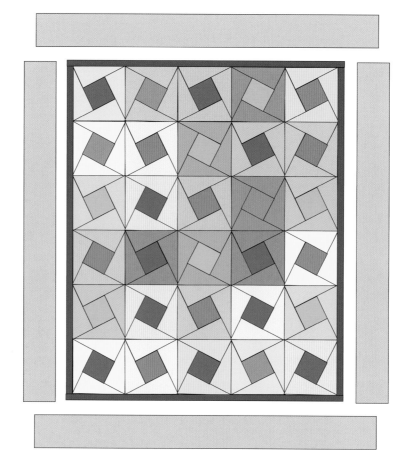

*With the gorgeous rose-themed fabric used in the quilt, particularly in the border, we couldn't resist using one of our favourite quilting patterns called Maggie's Rose.*

*In our variation, we used a fun range Bungle Jungle by Moda. Instead of using four dark strips for the block centres we bought an extra yard/metre of animal fabric and fussy cut 5in squares for the block centres. This meant that we had four dark strips spare and we cut these into 2½in x 42in strips to make a scrappy binding. We therefore only needed a long quarter to cut six 1½in strips for the inner border. Once you have the basic pattern you can personalize your quilt so it becomes truly unique to you. The quilt was made by Vivian de Lang and longarm quilted by The Quilt Room.*

# MARMALADE CAKE

We used the pretty range called Marmalade by Bonnie & Camille for Moda, so this seemed the natural choice of name for this quilt. Apart from pulling four of the lightest dessert roll strips from the bundle, there is very little sorting needed for this quilt. The gorgeous variety of fabrics comes from the dessert roll and we have added a light background fabric and dark accent. It certainly makes choosing fabrics for a quilt a breeze. This makes a good size quilt and an extra border could be added to increase the size further.

For the variation quilt we used a luscious floral range of fabrics, with a rich purple accent to create a dramatic and impressive quilt.

*Recipe:*

## Marmalade Cake

This easy cake is deliciously moist, with lots of fresh, tangy orange flavours.

### Ingredients

- 6oz (170g) soft margarine
- 6oz (170g) golden caster sugar
- 3 large eggs
- Zest and juice of a large orange (reserve the juice for the icing)
- 3½oz (100g) orange marmalade
- 6oz (170g) self-raising flour
- 4oz (120g) icing sugar (for the icing)

Cream the margarine and sugar. Add the beaten eggs a little at a time. Add the orange zest and marmalade. Fold in the sieved flour. Place the mixture in a 2lb (900g) lined loaf tin and bake for 40 minutes at 180°C/350°F (gas mark 4). Top with icing made from the icing sugar mixed with sufficient orange juice to get the correct consistency.

# MARMALADE CAKE QUILT

## Vital Statistics

| | |
|---|---|
| Quilt size: | 81in x 81in |
| Block size: | 13½in |
| Number of blocks: | 36 |
| Setting: | 6 x 6 blocks |

## Requirements

- One dessert roll **OR** twenty 5in strips cut across the width of the fabric
- Five light fabrics ½yd (0.5m) of each **OR** an assortment of fourteen 5in strips cut across the fabric width
- 1½yd (1.25m) of dark accent fabric
- ⅝yd (60cm) of fabric for binding
- Multi-Size 45/90 ruler or similar tool for cutting half-square triangles from strips

## SORTING THE STRIPS

- Choose three of the lightest strips in the dessert roll to be light strips.
- Choose seventeen strips in the dessert roll to be medium strips.

## CUTTING INSTRUCTIONS

*Dessert roll strips:*
- Take the seventeen medium dessert roll strips and cut each strip into eight 5in squares to make a total of 136 squares. You need 132, so four are spare.
- Leave the three light dessert roll strips uncut.

*Light fabric:*
- If you are using half yards/metres, cut fourteen 5in strips across the width of the fabric.
- Subcut twelve strips into eight 5in squares to make a total of ninety-six.
- Leave two strips uncut to add to the three light dessert roll strips to make a total of five light 5in strips uncut.

*Dark fabric:*
- Cut nine 5in strips across the width of the fabric.
- Take four strips and subcut each strip into eight 5in squares to make a total of thirty-two dark 5in squares.
- Leave the remaining five dark strips uncut.

*Binding fabric:*
- Cut eight 2½in wide strips across the width of the fabric

MARMALADE CAKE

## MAKING THE HALF-SQUARE TRIANGLES

**1** Take a 5in light strip and a 5in dark strip and press right sides together ensuring that they are exactly one on top of the other. The pressing will help hold the two strips together.

**2** Lay them out on a cutting mat and position the Multi-Size 45/90 ruler as shown in the diagram, lining up the 4½in mark at the bottom edge of the strips. Trim the selvedge and cut the first triangle. You will notice that the cut-out triangle has a flat top. This would just have been a dog ear you needed to cut off, so it is saving you time.

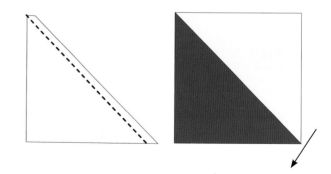

**3** Rotate the ruler 180 degrees as shown and cut the next triangle. Continue along the strip cutting the required amount of triangles. Cut fourteen triangles from each strip.

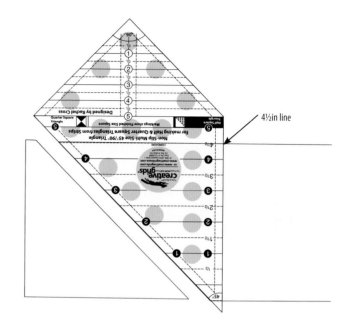

**4** Sew along the diagonal of each pair of triangles. Trim the dog ears and press open towards the dark fabric to form fourteen dark and light half-square triangle units. Repeat with all five light 5in strips and five dark 5in strips to make a total of seventy light and dark half-square triangle units. You need sixty-four, so six are spare.

6 Repeat this process to make a total of thirty-two split nine-patch blocks. Press as shown.

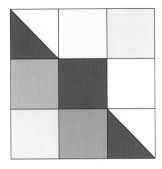

Make 32

## ASSEMBLING THE BLOCKS

5 Take three light squares, three medium squares, one dark square and two half-square triangle units and sew them together in the layout shown in the diagram to make one block. Press the rows of the block in the directions shown.

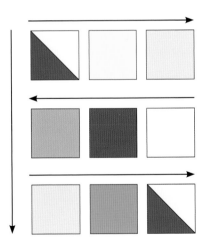

**7** Take nine medium squares and sew them together to make a nine-patch block. Press the seams as shown.

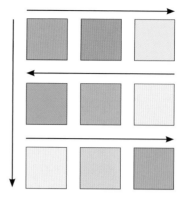

**8** Repeat this process to make a total of four nine-patch blocks for the quilt.

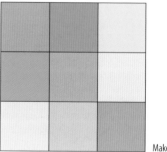

Make 4

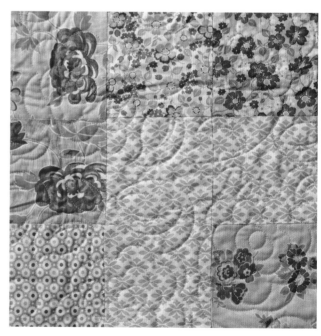

# ASSEMBLING THE QUILT

**9** Referring to the quilt diagram lay out the blocks, rotating the blocks to create the pattern as shown. When you are happy with the layout sew the blocks into rows and then sew the rows together.

**10** The quilt top is now complete. Prepare the top, wadding (batting) and backing fabric for quilting and quilt as desired – see Quilting in the General Techniques section. Bind the quilt to finish, following the instructions in Binding a Quilt.

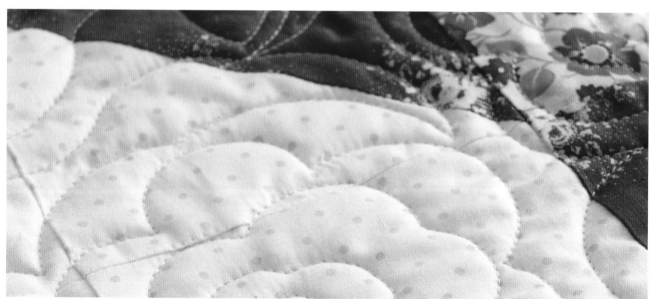

*We chose a lovely rose quilting pattern with details of leaves and this can be seen clearly in both the background and the blocks.*

Our variation uses the Henley Flower range by Makower and we have added a deep purple accent fabric for a bold look. It would be easy to increase the overall size of the quilt by adding some borders – perhaps a plain inner border and a pieced squares outer border. This quilt was made by the authors and longarm quilted by The Quilt Room.

# PARADISE

The traditional Friendship Star block lends itself perfectly to a dessert roll as you can create the squares and half-square triangle units easily from each 5in strip. We added extra light fabrics to the dessert roll and created a good size quilt without any wastage of fabric. Ticklish is the name of this dessert roll from Me & My Sister and we love the bright and sunny colouring.

The variation quilt uses a more traditional colour palette reproduced from the American Civil War period to create a beautiful quilt that would be at home in most decors.

*Recipe:*

## Paradise Cake
A delicious cake filled with nuts and fruits and snuggled on a bed of apricot jam – yum!

### Ingredients
- Ready-made short-crust pastry
- Apricot jam
- 6oz (170g) margarine
- 6oz (170g) caster sugar
- 2 eggs
- 3oz (85g) ground almonds
- 3oz (85g) chopped cherries
- 2½oz (70g) chopped nuts
- 9oz (250g) dried fruit

Line a large swiss roll tin with the pastry and spread with jam. Cream the margarine and sugar together and then beat in the eggs. Add the other ingredients and then spread the mixture over the jam. Bake for 25 minutes at 180°C/350°F (gas mark 4).

# PARADISE QUILT

## Vital Statistics

Quilt size:          63in x 76½in
Block size:          13½in
Number of blocks:    20
Setting:             4 x 5 blocks + 4½in border

## Requirements

- One dessert roll **OR** twenty 5in strips cut across the width of the fabric
- Five light fabrics ½yd (0.5m) of each **OR** an assortment of fifteen 5in light strips cut across the fabric width
- 1yd (1m) of fabric for border
- The binding is made from spare light fabric
- Multi-Size 45/90 ruler or other speciality tool for making half-square triangles from strips

## SORTING THE STRIPS

- Artistic licence can be used here but the design does work better if the four strips allocated to be light are lighter than the rest.
- Choose ten of the darkest strips to be the large stars.
- Choose four of the lightest strips to become light.
- The six remaining strips will be medium.

## CUTTING INSTRUCTIONS

*Dessert roll strips:*
- From each of the ten darkest dessert roll strips cut two 5in squares. These are the centres of the large stars and will be matched up with the half-square triangles later. Leave the balance of the strips uncut.
- Leave the four light strips and six medium strips uncut.

*Light fabric:*
- Cut each of the five half yards of light fabric into three 5in strips across the width of the fabric to make a total of fifteen 5in strips. Add these strips to the four light dessert roll strips to make a total of nineteen light 5in strips.

*Border fabric:*
- Cut six 5in strips across the width of the fabric.
- Take three of the 5in border strips and cut each strip into eight 5in squares. You need twenty, so four are spare.
- Leave the remaining three border strips uncut.

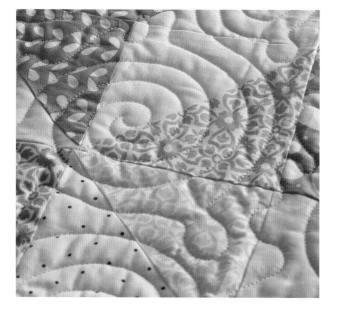

## MAKING THE HALF-SQUARE TRIANGLES

**1** Take a 5in medium dessert roll strip and a 5in light strip and press right sides together, ensuring that they are exactly one on top of the other. The pressing will help hold the two strips together.

**2** Lay them out on a cutting mat and position the Multi-Size 45/90 ruler as shown in the diagram, lining up the 4½in mark at the bottom edge of the strips. Trim the selvedge and cut the first triangle. You will notice that the cut-out triangle has a flat top. This would just have been a dog ear you needed to cut off, so it is saving you time.

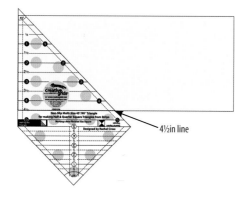

4½in line

**3** Rotate the ruler 180 degrees as shown and cut the next triangle. Continue along the pair of strips, cutting fourteen triangles from each pair of strips.

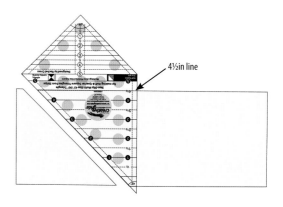

4½in line

**4** Sew along the diagonal of each pair of triangles. Trim the dog ears and press open towards the medium fabric to form fourteen medium and light half-square triangle units. Repeat with all six medium 5in strips and six light 5in strips to make a total of eighty-four medium and light half-square triangle units. You need eighty, so four are spare.

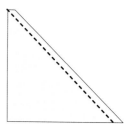

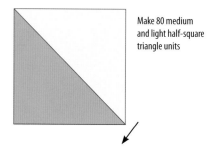

Make 80 medium and light half-square triangle units

**5** Repeat steps 1–4 with the ten dark dessert roll strips and ten light strips. The dark strips now measure only 32in so are shorter than your light strips. Cut eight triangles from each pair of strips to make a total of eighty light and dark half-square triangle units. Set the balance of the light strip aside for the binding. The balance of the dark strip is spare.

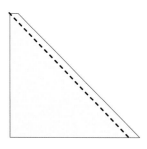

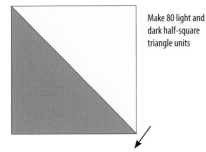

Make 80 light and dark half-square triangle units

**6** Repeat steps 1–4 with the three 5in strips from the border fabric and three light strips. You only need to cut twelve pairs of triangles from each strip to make a total of thirty-six half-square triangle units. Set these aside for the border.

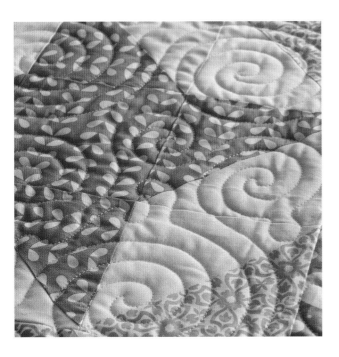

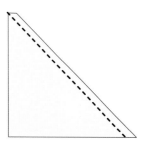

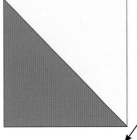

Make 36 half-square triangle units for the border

## ASSEMBLING THE BLOCKS

**7** Choose four dark and light half-square triangle units from the same fabric and match up with the 5in square of the same fabric.

**8** Choose four medium and light half-square triangle units. We used the same medium fabric in our blocks but they can be varied if you choose.

**9** Sew the units into rows and then sew the rows together, pressing as shown in the diagram.

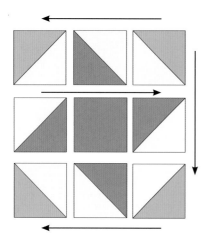

## ASSEMBLING THE QUILT

**10** Referring to the quilt diagram lay out the blocks as shown. When you are happy with the layout sew the blocks into rows and then sew the rows together. Press the seams. If you rotate alternate blocks 180 degrees the seams will nest together nicely.

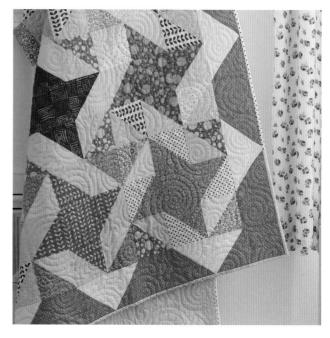

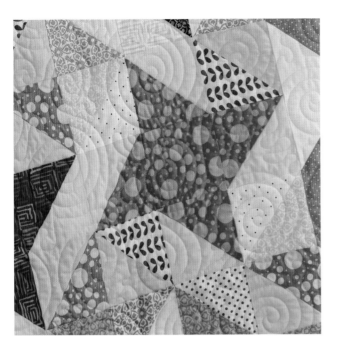

## ADDING THE BORDERS

**13** Pin and sew the side borders to the quilt, easing if necessary. Press the seams.

**14** Pin and sew the top and bottom borders to the top and bottom of the quilt and press.

## SEWING THE BORDERS

**11** Take five 5in border squares and ten border half-square triangle units and sew together as shown in the diagram to make one side border. Repeat to make another side border.

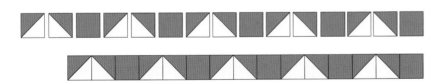

**12** Take six 5in border squares and eight half-square triangle units and sew together as shown to make the top border. Repeat to make the bottom border.

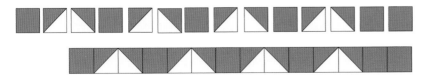

**15** The quilt top is now complete. Prepare the top, wadding (batting) and backing fabric for quilting and quilt as desired – see Quilting in the General Techniques section. Bind the quilt to finish, following the instructions in Binding a Quilt.

To make a scrappy binding, collect up the light strips set aside for the binding, which are approximately 5in x 17in. Cut them in half lengthways to make rectangles 2½in x 17in approximately. Sew them into a continuous length to make a length of at least 300in.

*This is a contemporary, fun quilting pattern called Sticky Buns, which matches perfectly with the fun fabrics used in this quilt.*

*In contrast to the sunny colouring of our main quilt we used a reproduction American Civil War range for our variation. It's amazing how different the effect is, and how cosy the quilt looks. You can imagine snuggling underneath this quilt by the fire on a cold evening. This quilt was made by the authors and longarm quilted by The Quilt Room.*

# SEVENTH HEAVEN

A black background can sometimes be the perfect accompaniment to a range of fabrics and here it creates a dramatic quilt with the Lark fabric range by Amy Butler. We created the design using flip-over corners, which we love. We just mark the square with a fold just before sewing and with the help of lots of chain piecing the quilt speeds together in no time. With seven blocks across and seven blocks down, this was one of our easiest quilts to name!

The choice of background plays a big part, especially in this quilt design, and in our variation quilt we have shown you how stylish it looks with a lighter colour.

## Recipe:

### Seventh Heaven Chocolate Cake

You will definitely feel you are in seventh heaven once you have tasted this chocolate cake!

### Ingredients
- 10oz (300g) caster sugar
- 4oz (120g) soft margarine
- 2 eggs
- 6oz (180g) plain flour
- 1 teaspoon of bicarbonate of soda
- ¼ teaspoon baking powder
- 2oz (60g) cocoa powder
- 7 fl oz (200ml) cold water
- 9oz (250g) dried fruit

### Icing
- 2oz (60g) caster sugar
- 1½oz (45g) butter
- 2 tablespoons of water
- 3oz (90g) icing sugar
- 1oz (30g) cocoa powder

Cream the sugar and margarine and beat in the eggs. Sieve the flour, baking powder and bicarbonate of soda into the mixture. Mix the cocoa and water together and add to the mixture. Put into two lined 9in (23cm) tins and bake at 180°C/350°F (gas mark 4) for around 25 minutes. For the icing, melt caster sugar, butter and water but do not boil. Pour onto the icing sugar and cocoa. Stir occasionally while it cools and thickens. Spread in the centre and on top of the cake.

# Seventh Heaven Quilt

## Vital Statistics

Quilt size: 58½in x 76½in
Block size: 4½in x 9in
Number of blocks: 49
Setting: 7 vertical rows of 7 blocks with a 2¼in sashing + 4½in pieced border

## Requirements

- One dessert roll **OR** twenty 5in strips cut across the width of the fabric
- 3yd (2.75m) of fabric for background
- ½yd (50cm) of fabric for binding

## SORTING THE STRIPS

- Choose thirteen strips for the rectangles.
- Choose seven strips for the border.

## CUTTING INSTRUCTIONS

*Dessert roll strips:*
- Take the thirteen strips allocated for the rectangles and cut each strip into four rectangles 5in x 9½in to make a total of fifty-two. You need forty-nine, so three are spare.
- Take the seven strips allocated for the border and cut each strip into eight 5in squares. You need fifty-two, so four are spare.

*Background fabric:*
- Cut one 5in strip across the width of the fabric and subcut four 5in squares for the corners. The rest of the strip is spare.
- Cut thirteen 2¾in strips across the width of the fabric and subcut each strip into fifteen 2¾in squares to make 195 squares.
- Refold the fabric *lengthways* and cut fifteen 2¾in strips down the length of the fabric. Set ten aside for the sashing and border strips.
- Subcut five strips into 2¾in squares. You will get twenty-two from each lengthways strip to make 110. Add these to the 195 already cut. You need 300 in total, so five are spare.

*Binding:*
- Cut seven 2½in strips across the width of the fabric.

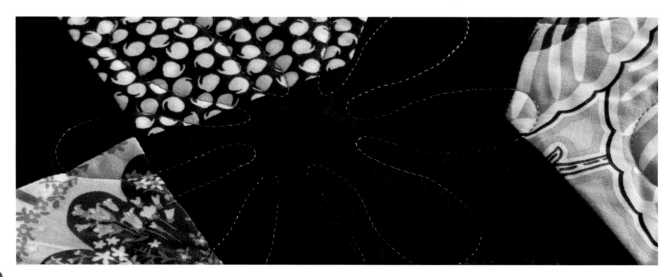

## MAKING THE BLOCKS

**1** Draw a diagonal line from corner to corner on the wrong side of a 2¾in background square or mark the diagonal line with a fold.

**2** With right sides together, lay a marked square on a corner of one of the 5in x 9½in rectangles, aligning the outer edges. Sew across the diagonal, using the marked diagonal line as the stitching line (shown in white on the diagram for clarity).

**3** Flip the square over and press towards the outside of the block. For those familiar with our books, we would normally say trim the excess fabric from the flip-over corner but do not trim the dessert roll rectangle. Although this creates a little more bulk, this will help keep your patchwork in shape. However, if you are using a light background fabric and you find that the darker fabric shows through the light fabric, it may be necessary to trim the dessert roll fabric as well. Do not trim the dessert roll fabric until you have pressed the flip-over corner and checked that it is sewn on accurately. If it is not sewn on perfectly then it is much better to leave the dessert roll rectangle uncut.

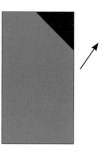

**4** Repeat and sew three other background squares on the remaining three corners.

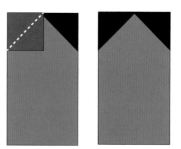

**5** Now make forty-nine rectangles with flip-over corners on all four corners.

Make 49

**6** Using the same technique sew two flip-over corners on to a 5in square, as shown. Repeat to make fifty-two squares with two flip-over corners.

Make 52

## ASSEMBLING THE QUILT

**7** Sew seven rectangles together to form one vertical row, pinning the centre points to ensure a perfect match. Press the seams. Repeat to make seven vertical rows.

**8** Measure the length of the vertical rows, which should be approximately 63½in, and trim eight sashing and border strips to that measurement. It is important that all eight sashing and border strips are cut to the same length.

**9** Sew a sashing strip to both sides of the first row and to the right of all the other rows, pinning and easing if necessary.

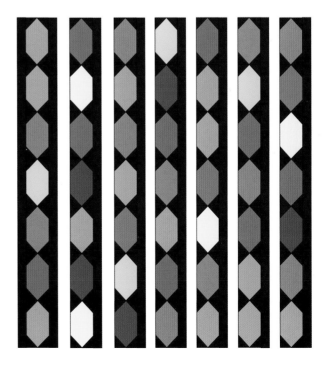

**10** When the sashing strips are sewn into place, sew all the vertical rows together and then press the seams.

**11** Measure the horizontal width across the quilt and trim the two remaining border strips to that measurement. Pin and sew to the top and bottom of the quilt and then press.

## ADDING THE PIECED BORDER

**12** Sew fifteen squares together to form a side border, as shown. Repeat to make the other side border.

**13** Sew eleven squares together and sew two 5in background squares to both ends to make the top border. Repeat to make the bottom border.

**14** Sew the side borders on first, pinning and easing where necessary. Press the seams. Now sew the top and bottom borders on, pinning and easing where necessary, and then press.

**15** The quilt top is now complete. Prepare the top, wadding (batting) and backing fabric for quilting and quilt as desired – see Quilting in the General Techniques section. Bind the quilt to finish, following the instructions in Binding a Quilt.

*For this quilt we chose a bold, quirky quilting pattern and used a bright variegated blue/green thread so the quilting design stood out on the various fabrics.*

*Our variation is made in the fabric range called Fellowship by Brannock & Patek, set against a neutral background fabric, which gives a wonderful country effect. This quilt was made by Yasmin Duggan, who is one of 'The Quilt Room Girls', and longarm quilted by The Quilt Room.*

# BLUEBERRY DELIGHT

Looking at this quilt it is hard to imagine that the design started out as a nine-patch block – oh how we love that block! Our main quilt and our variation quilt look totally different. In reality the only difference is that the border fabric in our main quilt is used to make the setting triangles in our variation, which are needed as in our variation we have set the blocks on point. One basic pattern can create lots of different effects, making it easy to create a quilt unique to you. Our dessert roll here is Aurora's Iris Garden by Brannock & Patek, full of gorgeous greens, ravishing reds and lovely lilacs. Having the fabrics so beautifully coordinated is a sure recipe for success.

## Recipe:

### Blueberry Delight

This is a wonderful cake – perfect for afternoon tea while quilting with friends.

### Ingredients
- 4oz (120g) butter
- 4oz (120g) caster sugar
- 2 large eggs
- 4oz (120g) self-raising flour

### Filling
- Whipped double cream
- Fresh blueberries

Cream the butter and sugar. In a separate bowl beat the eggs and add them a little at a time to the mixture. Fold in the sieved flour. Divide the mixture between two 7in (18cm) greased round sponge tins and bake for 25–30 minutes at 170°C/325°F (gas mark 3). When cool, sandwich the two layers together with the cream and blueberries. Sieve icing sugar on top to decorate (optional).

# BLUEBERRY DELIGHT QUILT

## Vital Statistics

Quilt size:        66in x 78in
Block size:        6in
Number of blocks:  120
Setting:           10 x 12 blocks + 3in border

## Requirements

- One dessert roll **OR** twenty 5in strips across the width of the fabric
- 2¼yd (2.10m) of additional fabric
- ⅞yd (75cm) of fabric for border
- ⅝yd (60cm) of fabric for binding

## SORTING THE STRIPS

- Choose two dark strips.
- Choose eight mediums strips.
- Choose eight lights strips.
- Two strips are spare.

## CUTTING INSTRUCTIONS

*Additional fabric:*
- Cut eleven 7in strips across the width of the additional fabric and subcut each strip into six 7in squares to make a total of sixty-six. You need sixty-four in total, so two are spare.

*Border fabric:*
- Cut seven 3½in wide strips across the width of the fabric.

*Binding fabric:*
- Cut eight 2½in wide strips across the width of the fabric.

*We used a traditional leaf pattern called Vicky's Leaves and chose a taupe thread, which blended well with all the different colours in this quilt.*

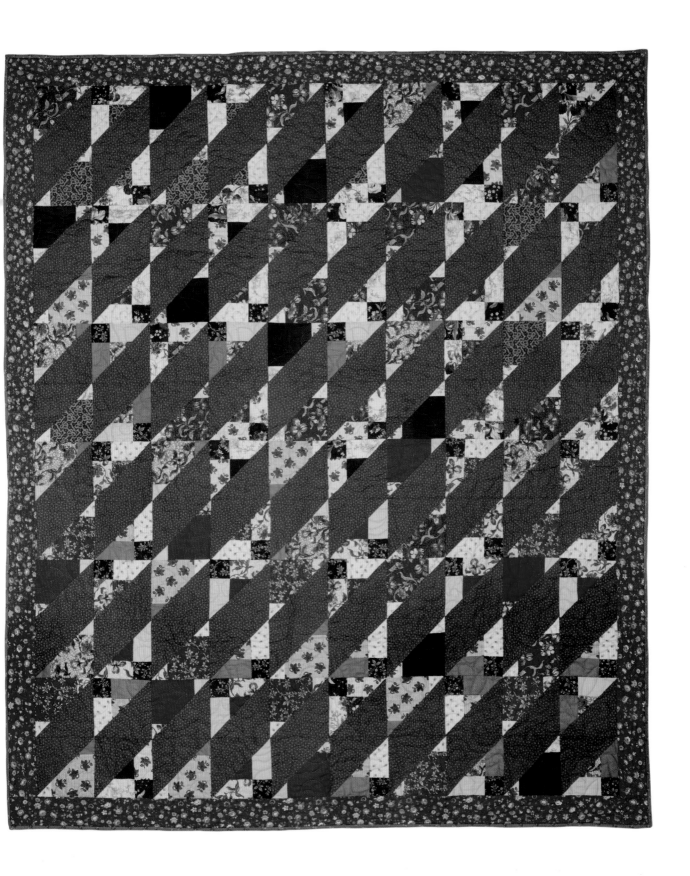

BLUEBERRY DELIGHT

# MAKING THE NINE-PATCH BLOCKS

**1** Choose two medium strips and one light strip and sew together as shown, with the light strip in the centre, to make one strip unit A. Repeat to make four of strip unit A in total. Press as shown.

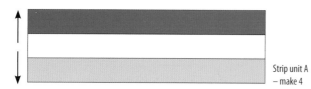

Strip unit A – make 4

**2** Choose two light strips and one dark strip and sew together as shown with the dark strip in the centre to make one strip unit B. Repeat to make two of strip unit B. Press as shown.

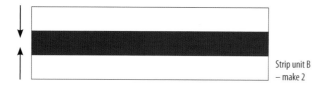

Strip unit B – make 2

**3** Place one unit B right sides together on a unit A, aligning the edges and making sure the seams are nesting up against each other.

**4** From the layered A and B units cut eight segments in total, each 5in wide.

**5** Sew the segments together as shown and press open. Repeat with another unit A and the remaining unit B to make sixteen units.

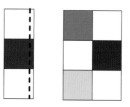

**6** Take the remaining two unit As and cut each strip unit into eight 5in segments to make a total of sixteen.

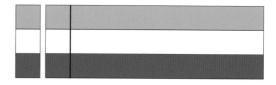

**7** Sew these segments to the units already sewn to create sixteen nine-patch blocks.

Make 16

## REARRANGING THE NINE-PATCH BLOCKS

**8** Working with one nine-patch block at a time, cut one nine-patch block accurately through the centre in each direction as shown to make four quarters. *Note:* the centre segment is 4½in wide so the best method of accurately cutting is to line up the 2¼in mark on your ruler on the seam line.

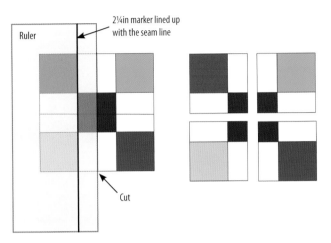

**9** On the reverse of one of these quarters, mark the diagonal line from light corner to light corner, as shown. Make sure you do not mark through the dark square.

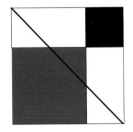

**10** Lay this unit right sides together on top of a 7in background square, aligning the edges. Pin to hold in place. Sew either side of the marked diagonal line, as shown, with a seam allowance no larger than a scant ¼in.

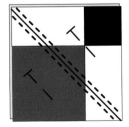

**11** Cut along the marked diagonal line and press as shown to reveal two different blocks – block A and block B.

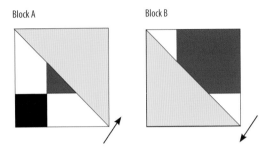

**12** Lay a quilting square over the blocks to check that each block measures 6½in. Trim if necessary. *Note:* if you find that your blocks are measuring under 6½in then your seam allowance when sewing either side of the diagonal marked line (step 10) is too large. A solution is to move the needle position on your machine to the right to make your seam allowance slightly narrower. You can always trim the excess if your block is over 6½in square but you don't want your blocks too small.

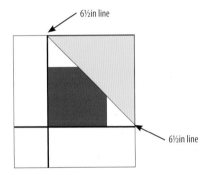

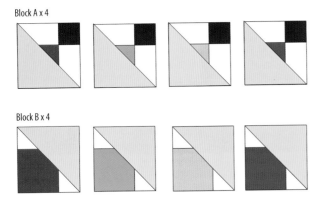

**13** Repeat with the other three quarters of the nine-patch block to make a total of four block A and four block B.

**Block A x 4**

**Block B x 4**

**14** Repeat steps 8–13 with all sixteen nine-patch blocks to create a total of 128 6½in blocks. You need sixty of block A and sixty of block B, so eight blocks will be spare.

## ASSEMBLING THE QUILT

**15** Lay out the blocks as shown, with each row having five A blocks and five B blocks. The blocks in row one have the large triangle at bottom right and the blocks in row two have the large triangle at top left.

**16** When you are happy with the layout sew the blocks into rows, pressing the seams of alternate rows in opposite directions so the seams will nest together nicely when sewing the rows together.

**17** Sew the rows together pinning at every seam intersection to ensure a perfect match.

**18** The quilt top is now complete. Prepare the top, wadding (batting) and backing fabric for quilting and quilt as desired – see Quilting in the General Techniques section. Bind the quilt to finish, following the instructions in Binding a Quilt.

# MAKING THE VARIATION QUILT

We set our variation quilt on point to show you how different the quilt can look with a different setting. The requirements are the same as the main quilt but here the fabric allocated for the border is now used to create the setting triangles. This quilt has no added border and its finished size is 69in square.

## CUTTING INSTRUCTIONS FOR BORDER/SETTING TRIANGLE FABRIC

- Cut two 10½in strips and subcut one strip into four 10½in squares and one strip into three 10½in squares, to make seven 10½in squares in total. Cut across both diagonals of the seven 10½in squares to create twenty-eight setting triangles.

- Cut one 6½in strip across the width of the fabric and subcut into two 6½in squares. Cut across one diagonal of each square to make four corner triangles. Cutting the setting and corner triangles in this way ensures there are no bias edges on your quilt.

## MAKING THE BLOCKS

1 Follow the instructions for the main quilt and create a total of 128 6½in blocks. You will only need sixty-four of block A and forty-nine of block B for this variation, so fifteen of block B are spare.

## ASSEMBLING THE QUILT

2 Create row one by sewing a setting triangle to both sides of one block A. The setting triangles are cut slightly larger to make the blocks 'float', so when sewing the setting triangles make sure the bottom of the triangle is aligned with the bottom of the block. Press towards block A.

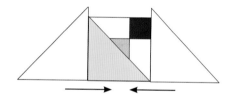

3 Create row two by alternating two block As with one block B and sewing a setting triangle to both ends.

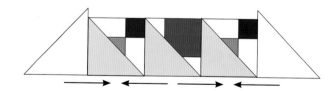

4 Referring to the variation quilt layout diagram, continue to sew the blocks into rows, alternating blocks A and B and sewing a setting triangle to both ends. Always press towards block A and your seams will nest together nicely when sewing the rows together.

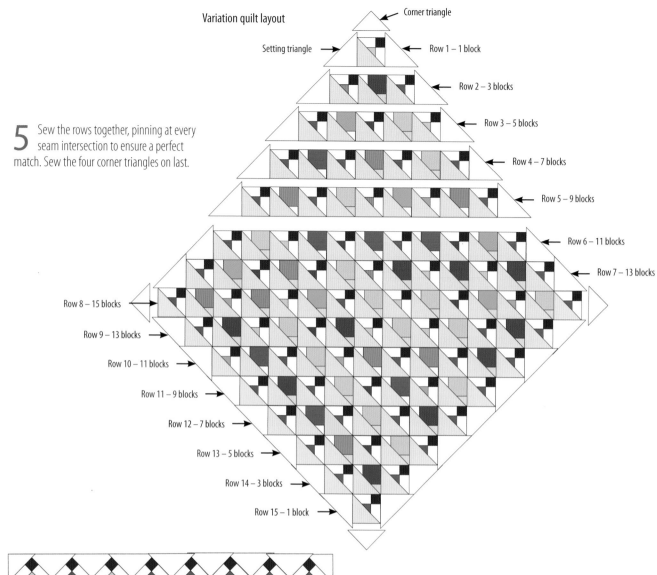

Variation quilt layout

Corner triangle

Setting triangle → Row 1 – 1 block

Row 2 – 3 blocks

**5** Sew the rows together, pinning at every seam intersection to ensure a perfect match. Sew the four corner triangles on last.

Row 3 – 5 blocks

Row 4 – 7 blocks

Row 5 – 9 blocks

Row 6 – 11 blocks

Row 7 – 13 blocks

Row 8 – 15 blocks →

Row 9 – 13 blocks →

Row 10 – 11 blocks →

Row 11 – 9 blocks →

Row 12 – 7 blocks →

Row 13 – 5 blocks →

Row 14 – 3 blocks →

Row 15 – 1 block →

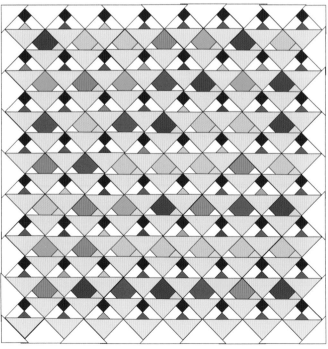

**6** The variation quilt top is now complete. Prepare the top, wadding (batting) and backing fabric for quilting and quilt as desired – see Quilting in the General Techniques section. Bind the quilt to finish, following the instructions in Binding a Quilt.

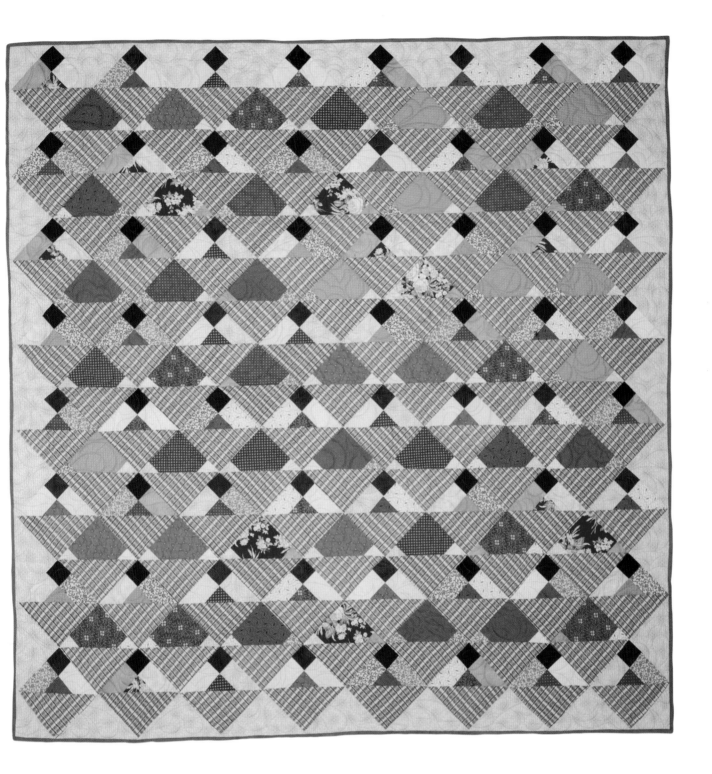

*Our variation uses a reproduction American Civil War range from Marcus Brothers. Setting the blocks on point creates a totally different effect from the main quilt. This quilt was made by the authors and longarm quilted by The Quilt Room.*

# HEN PARTY

We have six very productive chickens and when Nicky's three-year-old son Freddie comes to stay his first job of the morning is to go out and collect the eggs. Our hens are all an ordinary brown colour (although we wouldn't say that in front of them) and we think they would be very proud being depicted in the gorgeous colouring of Chateau Rouge by French General. We give requirements and instructions for twenty hen blocks and these twenty blocks can be used for your quilt. However, we felt the hens needed somewhere to live so our hen house block is optional.

If you want even more colourful hens try our variation quilt, which uses the bright colours and patterns of Kaffe Fassett fabrics.

## Recipe:

### Crème Brûlée

Our recipe for this quilt has to be our all-time favourite dessert, which we always make when we have an abundance of lovely free-range eggs.

### Ingredients
- 2 cups (1 pint/570mls) fresh double cream
- 4 egg yolks
- 3oz (90g) caster sugar
- 1 teaspoon vanilla essence

Beat the egg yolks, 60g (2oz) of caster sugar and vanilla essence. Put the cream in a heatproof bowl over a pan of hot water and bring to *just below* boiling point (don't boil). Pour the hot cream into the mixture and stir. Pour into a shallow baking dish and place in a roasting tin half full of hot water. Bake in a cool oven (150°C/300°F or gas mark 2) for an hour or until set. Remove from the tin and place in the fridge for several hours or overnight. Sprinkle the top with the remaining sugar and put under a preheated hot grill until the sugar turns to caramel (don't burn it). Leave to cool before serving.

# Hen Party Quilt

## Vital Statistics

| | |
|---|---|
| Quilt size: | 50in x 62½in |
| Block size: | 12½in |
| Number of blocks: | 20 |
| Setting: | 4 x 5 blocks |

## Requirements

- One dessert roll **OR** twenty 5in strips cut across the width of the fabric
- 1½yd (1.4m) of fabric for background
- ¼yd (25cm) of red fabric
- ½yd (50cm) of fabric for binding
- Black felt or black embroidery thread for eyes and feet
- Multi-Size 45/90 ruler or similar tool for making half-square triangles from strips (only required if making the optional hen house block)

## SORTING THE STRIPS

- Each dessert roll strip will make one hen and one frame.

## CUTTING INSTRUCTIONS

*Dessert roll strips:*
- Keeping the pieces from each of the twenty dessert roll strips in separate piles, cut each strip as follows.
    – One 5in x 5in square.
    – Two 2½in x 9in rectangles.
    – Two 2½in x 13in rectangles.
    – One 2½in x 7in rectangle.
    – Two 2½in x 2½in squares.

| 5in x 5in | 2½in x 9in | 2½in x 13in | 2½in x 7in | 8in x 5in spare – two used for hen house block |
|---|---|---|---|---|
| | 2½in x 9in | 2½in x 13in | | |

2½in x 2½in    2½in x 2½in    Spare

*Red fabric:*
- Cut three 1½in strips across the width of the fabric and subcut into sixty 1½in squares.

*Background fabric:*
- Cut six 2½in strips across the width of the fabric and subcut to make the following.
    – Twenty 2½in x 5in rectangles.
    – Forty 2½in x 2½in squares.
- Cut twenty 1½in strips across the width of the fabric and subcut as follows.
    – Two strips into twenty 1½in x 2½in rectangles.
    – Two strips into twenty 1½in x 3½in rectangles.
    – Three strips into twenty 1½in x 5in rectangles.
    – Four strips into twenty 1½in x 6in rectangles.
    – Four strips into twenty 1½in x 7in rectangles.
    – Five strips into twenty 1½in x 9in rectangles.
- Cut one 4¾in wide strip and set aside for the optional hen house block.

*Binding fabric:*
- Cut six 2½in strips across the width of the fabric.

*A simple meander is sometimes the perfect quilting choice. We quilted quite densely and used a blending thread, as we didn't want to detract from our beautiful hens!*

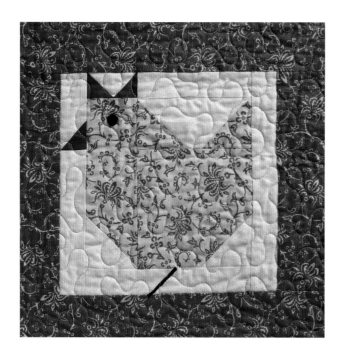

**3** Flip the square over and press towards the outside of the block to form unit A. Trim the excess fabric from the flip-over corner but do not trim the dessert roll square. Although this creates a little more bulk, this will help keep your patchwork in shape.

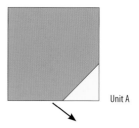

Unit A

**4** Draw a diagonal line from corner to corner on the wrong side of one of the 2½in dessert roll squares and sew to one end of a 2½in x 5in background rectangle as shown. Flip open and press.

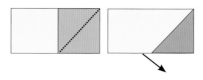

**5** Sew the remaining 2½in dessert roll square to the other end and press to form unit B.

Unit B

## MAKING A LEFT-FACING HEN BLOCK

**1** You need to make eight of the left-facing hen blocks in total. Working with one pile of dessert roll fabrics, draw a diagonal line from corner to corner on the wrong side of a 2½in background square, or mark the diagonal line with a fold.

**2** With right sides together, lay a marked square on the bottom-right corner of one of the 5in dessert roll squares, aligning the outer edges. Sew across the diagonal, using the marked diagonal line as the stitching line.

**6** With right sides together, sew unit B to unit A and then press as shown in the diagram.

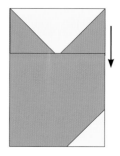

**7** Sew a 1½in x 5in background rectangle to the top of this unit to form unit C. Press as shown.

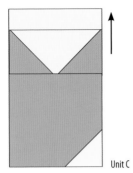

Unit C

**8** Using the same flip and sew method, sew a 2½in background square to the bottom left of a 2½in x 7in dessert roll rectangle to make unit D. Press and trim the excess background fabric.

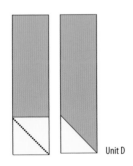

Unit D

**9** Using the same flip and sew method, sew two 1½in red squares to both ends of a 1½in x 2½in background rectangle to make unit E. Press and trim the excess red fabric.

 Unit E

**10** Now, with right sides together, sew unit E to unit D and then press as shown.

**11** Take units D and E and sew to the left-hand side of unit C and then press as shown.

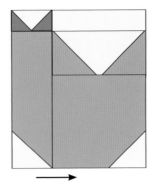

**12** Sew a 1½in x 7in background rectangle to the bottom of this unit to make unit F and press.

Unit F

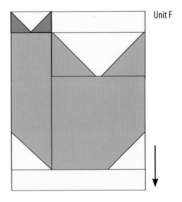

**13** Using the same flip and sew method, sew one 1½in red square to the bottom right of a 1½in x 3½in background rectangle. Press and then trim the excess red fabric.

**14** Now sew this unit to a 1½in x 6in background rectangle to make unit G.

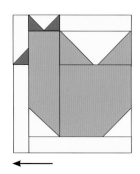

Unit G

**15** Take unit G and sew it to the left-hand side of unit F and then press as shown.

**16** Sew a 1½in x 9in background rectangle to the right-hand side and press as shown.

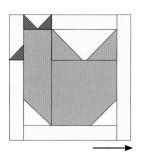

## MAKING A RIGHT-FACING HEN BLOCK

**17** You will need eleven of these if you are making the hen house block or twelve if all your blocks are going to be hen blocks. Working with one pile of dessert roll fabrics, draw a diagonal line from corner to corner on the wrong side of a 2½in background square or mark the diagonal line with a fold.

**18** With right sides together, lay a marked square on the bottom-left corner of one of the 5in dessert roll squares, aligning the outer edges. Sew across the diagonal, using the marked diagonal line as the stitching line.

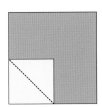

**19** Flip the square over and press towards the outside of the block. Trim the excess fabric from the flip-over corner but do not trim the dessert roll square. Although this creates a little more bulk, it will help keep your patchwork in shape.

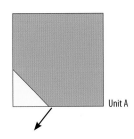

Unit A

**20** Draw a diagonal line from corner to corner on the wrong side of one of the 2½in dessert roll squares and sew to one end of a 2½in x 5in background rectangle as shown. Flip open and press.

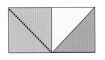

**21** Sew the remaining 2½in dessert roll square to the other end and press to form unit B.

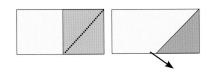

Unit B

**22** With right sides together, sew unit B to unit A and press in the direction shown.

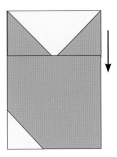

**23** Sew a 1½in x 5in background rectangle to the top of this unit to form unit C. Press as shown.

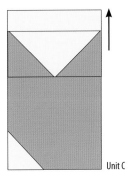

Unit C

**24** Using the same flip and sew method, sew a 2½in background square to the bottom right of a 2½in x 7in dessert roll rectangle to make unit D. Press and trim the excess background fabric.

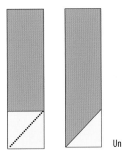

Unit D

**25** Using the same flip and sew method, sew two 1½in red squares to both ends of a 1½in x 2½in background rectangle to make unit E. Press and then trim the excess red fabric.

Unit E

**26** With right sides together sew unit E to unit D. Press as shown in the diagram.

**27** Take units D and E and sew to the right-hand side of unit C and then press.

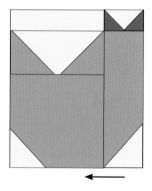

**28** Sew a 1½in x 7in background rectangle to the bottom of this unit to make unit F and press.

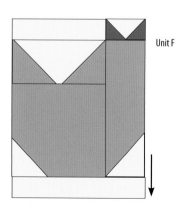
Unit F

**29** Using the same flip and sew method, sew one 1½in red square to the bottom left of a 1½in x 3½in background rectangle. Press and then trim the excess red fabric.

**30** Now sew this unit to a 1½in x 6in background rectangle to make unit G.

Unit G

**31** Sew unit G to the right-hand side of unit F and then press in the direction shown.

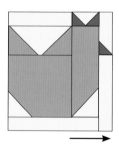

**32** Sew a 1½in x 9in background rectangle to the left-hand side and press.

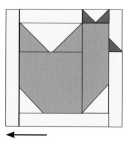

## ADDING THE BLOCK FRAMES

You can use rectangles of the same fabric as your hens or swap the frames around for a scrappier effect as we did.

**33** Sew two 2½in x 9in rectangles to both sides of the block and press. Sew the two 2½in x 13in rectangles to the top and bottom of the block and press. Repeat with the eight left-facing hen blocks and eleven right-facing hen blocks. Do not make the twelfth right-facing hen block if you are making the hen house block as you need the frames for the house block.

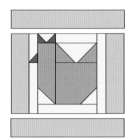

Make 8

**34** Appliqué or glue on ½in (1cm) circles of black felt for the eyes and embroider or machine sew a straight line for the feet.

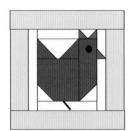

Make 11
(or 12 if not making
the hen house block)

## MAKING THE HEN HOUSE BLOCK

This block is optional and could be replaced by a hen block.

**35** Take the 4¾in wide background strip and cut one 4¾in x 8in rectangle and two 4¾in x 2¾in rectangles.

**36** Choose one of the spare 5in x 8in dessert roll rectangles and trim to measure 4¾in wide. Place it right sides together on the 4¾in x 8in background rectangle, aligning the edges. Lay them out on a cutting mat and position the Multi-Size 45/90 ruler as shown in the diagram, lining up the 4¼in mark at the bottom edge of the strips. If your ruler does not have this line marked then line it up halfway between the 4in and the 4½in line. Trim the selvedge and cut the first triangle.

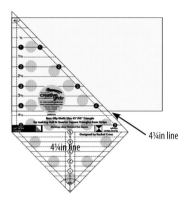

4¼in line

**37** Rotate the Multi-Size 45/90 ruler 180 degrees as shown and then cut the next triangle.

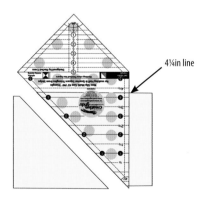

4¼in line

**38** Sew along the diagonal of both pairs of triangles. Trim the dog ears and press the seams of each triangle in opposite directions.

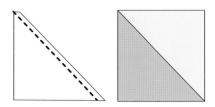

**39** With right sides together sew the triangles together. This makes the roof of the hen house.

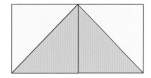

**40** From another spare dessert roll rectangle cut a square 4¾in x 4¾in. With right sides together, sew the 2¾in x 4¾in background rectangles to both sides.

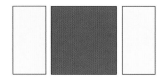

**41** Now sew this unit to the lower section of the roof section and then press.

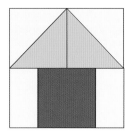

**42** Using the frames from the last dessert roll strip pile, sew to the block to complete. A ramp can be appliquéd into position using spare dessert roll strip fabric. We cut a 1½in x 3½in rectangle from spare fabric and pressed in the long sides. We then unpicked a few stitches and inserted the ramp into the correct position. Re-sew the seams and then hand appliqué the ramp to secure it.

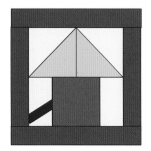

## ASSEMBLING THE QUILT

**43** Lay out your blocks with the hens facing to the right in the first, third and bottom rows and the hens facing to the left in the second and fourth rows. When you are happy with the arrangement sew the blocks together pinning at every seam intersection and then sew the rows together. Press the seams in alternate rows in opposite directions so the seams nest together nicely.

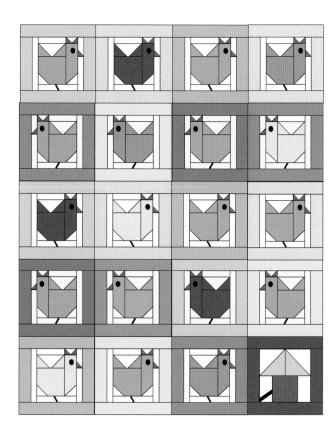

**44** The quilt top is now complete. Prepare the top, wadding (batting) and backing fabric for quilting and quilt as desired – see Quilting in the General Techniques section. Bind the quilt to finish, following the instructions in Binding a Quilt.

We have created even more exotic hens in our variation quilt and have used the bright fabrics of Kaffe Fassett. We also quilted this with an egg-shaped quilting pattern – are we mad? This quilt was made by the authors and longarm quilted by The Quilt Room.

# GENERAL TECHNIQUES

## TOOLS

All the projects in this book require rotary cutting equipment. You will need a self-healing cutting mat at least 18in x 24in and a rotary cutter. We recommend the 45mm or the 60mm diameter rotary cutter. Any rotary cutting work requires rulers and most people have a make they prefer. We like the Creative Grids rulers as their markings are clear, they do not slip on fabric and their Turn-a-Round facility is so useful when dealing with half-inch measurements. We recommend the 6½in x 24in as a basic ruler plus a large square no less than 12½in, which is handy for squaring up and making sure you are always cutting at right angles.

You do need a speciality ruler to cut half-square and quarter-square triangles from strips which you will find in the quilts Marmalade Cake, Paradise and Hen Party. Creative Grids have designed the Multi-Size 45/90 for us, which is perfect for the job. Rock 'n' Roll requires the use of a Multi-Size 45/60 or 60 degree triangle. Whichever ruler you decide to use, please make sure you are lining up your work on the correct markings.

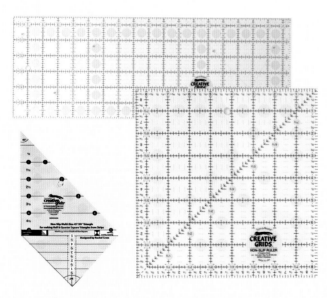

*We quilters all have our favourite rulers. We like to use the Creative Grids rulers and squares, some of which are shown here, including the Multi-Size 45/90.*

The Multi-Size 45/90 shows the *finished* size measurements. This means that when you are cutting half-square triangles from 2½in strips you line up the 2in marking along the bottom of the strip. This 2in marking relates to the fact that the finished half-square triangle unit will be 2in. If you are using a different ruler, please make sure you are lining up your work on the correct markings. The Easy Angle ruler for example shows the *unfinished* size and it will be the 2½in mark that will be lined up with the bottom of the strip.

## SEAMS

We cannot stress enough the importance of maintaining an accurate ¼in seam allowance throughout. We prefer to say an accurate *scant* ¼in seam because there are two factors to take into account. Firstly, the thickness of thread and secondly, when the seam allowance is pressed to one side it takes up a tiny amount of fabric. These are both extremely small amounts but if they are ignored you will find your *exact* ¼in seam allowance is taking up more than ¼in. So, it is well worth testing your seam allowance before starting on a quilt and most sewing machines have various needle positions that can be used to make any adjustments.

### SEAM ALLOWANCE TEST

Take a 2½in strip and cut off three segments each 1½in wide. Sew two segments together down the longer side and press the seam to one side. Sew the third segment across the top. It should fit exactly. If it doesn't, you need to make an adjustment to your seam allowance. If it is too long, your seam allowance is too wide and can be corrected by moving the needle on your sewing machine to the right. If it is too small, your seam allowance is too narrow and this can be corrected by moving the needle to the left.

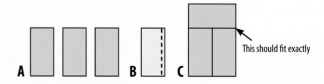

# Pressing

In quilt making, pressing is of vital importance and if extra care is taken you will be well rewarded. This is especially true when dealing with strips. If your strips start bowing and stretching you will lose accuracy.

• Always set your seam after sewing by pressing the seam as sewn, without opening up your strips. This eases any tension and prevents the seam line from distorting. Move the iron with an up and down motion, zigzagging along the seam rather than ironing down the length of the seam, which could cause distortion.

• Open up your strips and press on the right side of the fabric towards the darker fabric, if necessary guiding the seam underneath to make sure the seam is going in the right direction. Press with an up and down motion rather than along the length of the strip.

• Always take care if using steam and certainly don't use steam anywhere near a bias edge.

• When you are joining more than two strips together, press the seams after attaching each strip. You are more likely to get bowing if you leave it until your strip unit is complete before pressing.

• Each seam must be pressed flat before another seam is sewn across it. Unless there is a special reason for not doing so, seams are pressed towards the darker fabric. The main criteria when joining seams, however, is to have the seam allowances going in the opposite direction to each other as they then nest together without bulk. Your patchwork will lie flat and your seam intersections will be accurate.

# Pinning

Don't underestimate the benefits of pinning. When you have to align a seam it is important to insert pins to stop any movement when sewing. Long, fine pins with flat heads are recommended as they will go through the layers of fabric easily and allow you to sew up to and over them.

Seams should always be pressed in opposite directions so they will nest together nicely. Insert a pin either at right angles or diagonally through the seam intersection, ensuring that the seams are matching perfectly. When sewing, do not remove the pin too early as your fabric might shift and your seams will not be perfectly aligned.

# Chain Piecing

Chain piecing is the technique of feeding a series of pieces through the sewing machine without lifting the presser foot and without cutting the thread between each piece. Always chain piece when you can – it saves time and thread. Once your chain is complete, snip the thread between the pieces.

When chain piecing shapes other than squares and rectangles it is sometimes preferable when finishing one shape, to lift the presser foot slightly and reposition on the next shape, still leaving the thread uncut.

# REMOVING DOG EARS

A dog ear is the excess piece of fabric that overlaps past the seam allowance when sewing triangles to other shapes. Dog ears should always be cut off to reduce bulk. They can be trimmed using a rotary cutter, although snipping with small sharp scissors is quicker. Make sure you are trimming the points parallel to the straight edge of the triangle.

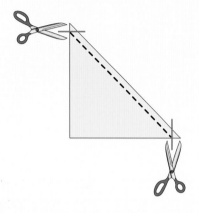

# JOINING BORDER AND BINDING STRIPS

If you need to join strips for your borders and binding, you may choose to join them with a diagonal seam to make them less noticeable. Press the seams open.

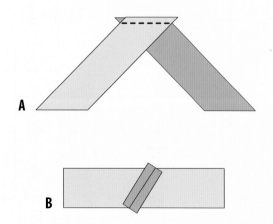

# ADDING BORDERS

The fabric requirements in this book all assume you are going to be sewing straight rather than mitred borders. If you intend to have mitred borders please add sufficient extra fabric for this.

## ADDING STRAIGHT BORDERS

**1** Determine the vertical measurement from top to bottom through the centre of your quilt top. Cut two side border strips to this measurement. Mark the halves and quarters of one quilt side and one border with pins. Placing right sides together and matching the pins, stitch the quilt and border together, easing the quilt side to fit where necessary. Repeat on the opposite side. Press open.

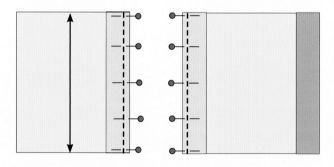

**2** Determine the horizontal measurement from side to side across the centre of the quilt top. Cut two top and bottom border strips to this measurement and add to the quilt top in the same manner.

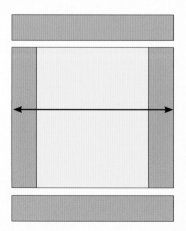

## Adding mitred borders

If you wish to create mitred borders rather than straight borders follow these instructions.

**1** Measure the length and width of the quilt and cut two border strips the length of the quilt plus twice the width of the border, and then cut two border strips the width of the quilt plus twice the width of the border.

**2** Sew the border strips to the quilt beginning and ending ¼in away from the corners, backstitching to secure at either end. Begin your sewing right next to where you have finished sewing your previous border but ensure your stitching doesn't overlap. When you have sewn your four borders, press and lay the quilt out on a flat surface, with the reverse side of the quilt up.

**3** Fold the top border up and align it with the side border. Press the resulting 45-degree line that starts at the ¼in stop and runs to the outside edge of the border.

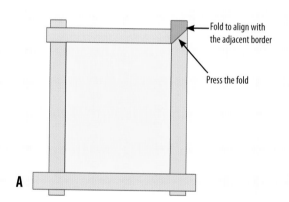

Fold to align with the adjacent border

Press the fold

**A**

**4** Now lift the side border above the top border and fold it to align with the top border. Press it to create a 45-degree line. Repeat with all four corners.

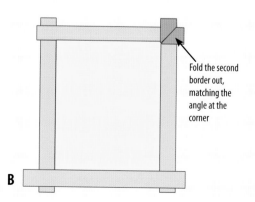

Fold the second border out, matching the angle at the corner

**B**

**5** Align the horizontal and vertical borders in one corner by folding the quilt diagonally and stitching along the pressed 45-degree line to form the mitre, backstitching at either end. Trim the excess border fabric ¼in from your sewn line. Repeat with the other three corners.

## Quilting

Quilting stitches hold the patchwork top, wadding (batting) and backing together and create texture over your finished patchwork. The choice is yours whether you hand quilt, machine quilt or use a longarm quilting service. There are many books dedicated to the techniques of hand and machine quilting but the basic procedure is as follows.

**1** With the aid of templates or a ruler, mark out the quilting lines on the patchwork top.

**2** Cut the backing fabric and wadding at least 4in larger all around than the patchwork top. Pin or tack (baste) the layers together securely to prepare them for quilting.

**3** Quilt either by hand or by machine. Remove any quilting marks on completion of the quilting.

## Binding a Quilt

The fabric requirements in this book are for a 2½in double-fold French binding cut on the straight grain.

**1** Trim the excess backing and wadding (batting) so that the edges are even with the top of the quilt.

**2** Join your binding strips into a continuous length (see Joining Border and Binding Strips), making sure there is sufficient to go around the quilt plus 8in–10in for corners and overlapping ends. With wrong sides together, press the binding in half lengthways. Fold and press under ½in to neaten edge at the end where you will start sewing.

**3** On the right side of the quilt and starting about 12in away from a corner, align the edges of the double thickness binding with the edge of the quilt so that the cut edges are towards the edges of the quilt and pin to hold in place. Sew with a ¼in seam allowance, leaving the first few inches open.

**4** At the first corner, stop ¼in from the edge of the fabric and backstitch (diagram A). Lift the needle and presser foot and fold the binding upwards (B). Fold the binding again but downwards. Stitch from the edge to ¼in from the next corner and repeat the turn (C).

**5** Continue all around the quilt, working each corner in the same way. When you come to the starting point, cut the binding, fold under the cut edge and overlap at the starting point.

**6** Fold the binding over to the back of the quilt and hand stitch in place, folding the binding at each corner to form a neat mitre.

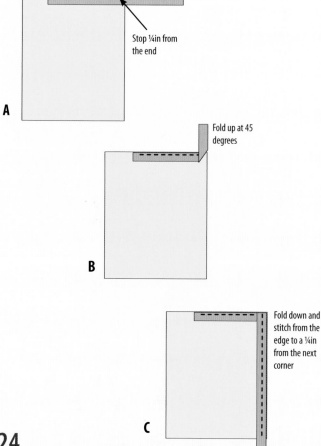

Stop ¼in from the end

**A**

Fold up at 45 degrees

**B**

Fold down and stitch from the edge to a ¼in from the next corner

**C**

# Making a Larger Quilt

If you want to make a larger version of any of the quilts in the book, refer to the Vital Statistics of the quilt, which shows the block size, the number of blocks, how the blocks are set, plus the size of border used. You can then calculate your requirements for a larger quilt.

# Setting on Point

Any block can take on a totally new look when set on point and you might like to try one of the quilts to see what it looks like on point. For this reason we have included information for setting quilts on point. Some people are a little daunted as there are a few things to take into consideration but here is all you need to know.

## How wide will my blocks be when set on point?

To calculate the measurement of the block from point to point multiply the size of the finished block by 1.414. Example: a 12in block will measure 12in x 1.414 which is 16.97in (just under 17in). Now you can calculate how many blocks you need for your quilt.

## How do I piece blocks on point?

Piece rows diagonally, starting at a corner. Triangles have to be added to the end of each row before joining the rows and these are called setting triangles.

## What size setting triangles do I cut?

Setting triangles form the outside of your quilt and need to have the straight grain on the outside edge to prevent stretching. To ensure this, these triangles are formed from quarter-square triangles, i.e., a square cut into four. The measurement for this is: Diagonal Block Size + 1¼in. Example: a 12in block (diagonal measurement approximately 17in) should be 18¼in.

Corners triangles are added last. They also need to have the outside edge on the straight grain so these should be cut from half-square triangles. To calculate the size of square to cut in half, divide the finished size of your block by 1.414 then add ⅞in. Example: a 12in block would be 12in divided by 1.414 = 8.49in + ⅞in (0.88) = 9.37in (or 9½in as it can be trimmed later).

Most diagonal quilts start off with one block and in each row thereafter the number of blocks increases by two. All rows contain an odd number of blocks. To calculate the quilt's finished size, count the number of diagonals across and multiply this by the diagonal measurement of the block. Do the same with the number of blocks down and multiply this by the diagonal measurement of the block.

If you want a rectangular quilt, count the number of blocks in the row that establishes the width and repeat that number in following rows to the desired length.

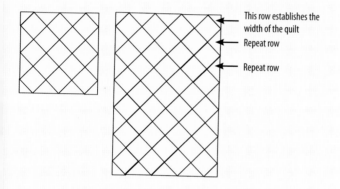

This row establishes the width of the quilt

Repeat row

Repeat row

# BACKING FABRIC

The patterns in this book do not include fabric requirements for backing as many people like to use extra wide backing fabric so they do not have to have any joins.

## USING 60IN WIDE FABRIC

This is a simple calculation as to how much you need to buy. Example: your quilt is 54in x 72in. Your backing needs to be at least 3in larger all round so your backing measurement is 60in x 78in. If you have found 60in wide backing, then you would buy the length, which is 78in. However, if you have found 90in wide backing, you can turn it round and you would only have to buy the width of 60in.

## USING 42IN WIDE FABRIC

You will need to have a join or joins in order to get the required measurement unless the backing measurement for your quilt is 42in or less on one side. If your backing measurement is less than 42in then you need only buy one length.

Using the previous example, if your backing measurement is 60in x 78in, you will have to have one seam somewhere in your backing. If you join two lengths of 42in fabric together your new fabric measurement will be 84in (less a little for the seam). This would be sufficient for the length of your quilt so you need to buy twice the width, i.e. 60in x 2 = 120in. Your seam will run horizontally.

If your quilt length is more than your new backing fabric measurement of 84in you will need to use the measurement of 84in for the width of your quilt and you will need to buy twice the length. Your seam will then run vertically.

# LABELLING YOUR QUILT

When you have finished your quilt it is important to label it even if the information you put on the label is just your name and the date. When looking at antique quilts it is always interesting to piece together information about the quilt, so you can be sure that any extra information you put on the label will be of immense interest to quilters of the future. For example, you could say why you made the quilt and who it was for, or for what special occasion.

Labels can be as ornate as you like, but a very simple and quick method is to write on a piece of calico with a permanent marker pen and then appliqué this to the back of your quilt.

# ABOUT THE AUTHORS

Pam Lintott opened her shop, The Quilt Room, in 1981, which she still runs today, along with her daughter Nicky. Pam is the author of *The Quilt Room Patchwork & Quilting Workshops,* as well as *The Quilter's Workbook.* The shop, together with the mail order department and longarm quilting department, is in a 15th century inn in the historic town of Dorking, Surrey, UK. *Dessert Roll Quilts* is Pam and Nicky's ninth book for David & Charles following on from their eight extremely successful Jelly Roll Quilt books including the phenomenally successful *Jelly Roll Quilts* and the last in the series, *Antique to Heirloom Jelly Roll Quilts.*

# ACKNOWLEDGMENTS

Pam and Nicky would first like to thank Mark Dunn and the whole team at Moda Fabrics for their continued support and for allowing them to use the name Dessert Roll in the title and throughout the book. Thanks to Janome Sewing Machines for allowing Pam and Nicky the use of their reliable sewing machines when making up the quilts for this book. Thanks to the efficient quilters from Cornwall who are always willing to test the patterns and thanks to Liz Lynch for her help and advice with the recipes. Thanks to the loyal team of staff at The Quilt Room, who keep The Quilt Room running smoothly when Pam and Nicky are rushing to meet tight deadlines. Last, but not least, special thanks to Pam's husband Nick and to Nicky's husband Rob for looking after sheep, hens, guinea fowl, dogs and a little boy, plus attending to everything else that needs to be done when deadlines are being met and computers and sewing machines are working overtime!

# USEFUL CONTACTS

**THE QUILT ROOM**
Shop & Mail Order
37–39 High Street, Dorking, Surrey RH4 1AR, UK
Tel: 01306 877307
www.quiltroom.co.uk

**MODA FABRICS/UNITED NOTIONS**
13800 Hutton Drive, Dallas, Texas 75234, USA
Tel: 800-527-9447
www.modafabrics.com

**CREATIVE GRIDS (UK) LIMITED**
23A Pate Road, Melton Mowbray, Leicestershire LE13 0RG, U
Tel: 01455 828667
www.creativegrids.com

**JANOME UK LTD.**
Janome Centre, Southside, Stockport, Cheshire SK6 2SP, UK
Tel: 0161 666 6011
www.janome.com

**STITCH CRAFT CREATE**
Brunel House, Newton Abbot, Devon TQ12 4PU, UK
Tel: 0844 8805852
www.stitchcraftcreate.co.uk

# INDEX

Names of manufacturers and product ranges are provided for
the information of readers, with no intention to infringe copyright
or trademarks.

A catalogue record for this book is available from the British Library.

ISBN-13: 978-1-4463-0354-2 paperback
ISBN-10: 1-4463-0354-3 paperback

Paperback edition printed in China by RR Donnelley for:
F&W Media International, Ltd
Brunel House, Forde Close, Newton Abbot, TQ12 4PU, UK

10 9 8 7 6 5 4 3 2 1

Acquisitions Editor: Sarah Callard
Junior Acquisitions Editor: James Brooks
Project Editor: Lin Clements
Designers: Marie-Claire Maine and Jennifer Stanley
Photographers: Jack Gorman and Simon Whitmore
Production Manager: Bev Richardson

F+W Media publishes high quality books on a wide range of subjects.
For more great book ideas visit: www.stitchcraftcreate.co.uk